For Lois & Bob

Our great non-Belgian heritage

Em & Russ

AF352119

ASSESS THE IRS!

Roger Whitely

VANTAGE PRESS
New York   Washington   Atlanta   Hollywood

FIRST EDITION

All rights reserved, including the right of
reproduction in whole or in part in any form.

Copyright © 1978 by Roger Whitely

Published by Vantage Press, Inc.
516 West 34th Street, New York, New York 10001

Manufactured in the United States of America
Standard Book Number 533-02946-5

Library of Congress Catalog Card Number 78-58274

DEDICATION

To those whose enterprise is thwarted by
   the Internal Revenue Service
To those who are harassed by it
To those who wish to fight it
To those who will enjoy a lampoon about it.

PREFACE

You, dear reader, if there be others than those receiving gratuitous copies, will find in Chapter I that this book was written during the end of 1974. Why is it now 1978? Well over a year was wasted trying to find a literary agent. Their excuses not to represent me were such as "overwhelmed with work," "pressures of present obligations." Not one answered, "I will not tackle that," and it may well be that the content of my abstracts sent to them was not a deterring factor. Turning next to publishers, with the help of friends, a member of one house did verbally imply that the publishing of such a book would not be in the best interests of his firm.

Then there are many months of lead time once a manuscript is accepted. This was increased since Vantage Press, Inc., correctly wanted releases by means of letters of permission from those fine persons, all all-American taxpayers, who by their affidavits had helped me overcome the Internal Revenue Service. I wish here to thank them for their original aid, as well as for the opportunity to use their letters in this novel.

It is now the summer of 1977, galley-proof time. You may properly ask, "Have the tax laws changed since your audit?" For you who are up or uptight on these matters, yes, they have. There were Congressional Acts in 1969 and in 1976 altering some of the laws, but not affecting this story in any fashion. Where the manuscript discusses breeding cattle, this commodity must be today in possession for longer periods of time before becoming depreciable. The Federal government has recently liberalized the laws regarding stock market losses so that a greater loss may be deducted.

The story is authentic. Names and addresses have been changed, even the name of a state. Chapter IV does depart from reality only in one sense. The arguments sent to an appellate conferee were in continuous form and the letters of support were attached in a bulk grouping as addenda. In this manuscript the affidavits are interwoven. Weaving requires some sewing and my needle work will be apparent from the number of stitch abscesses you will find.

CONTENTS

ASSESS THE IRS!

*LIFE IS MADE UP OF CONSTANT
    CALLS
TO ACTION, AND WE SELDOM
    HAVE TIME
FOR MORE THAN
    HASTILY CONTRIVED
ANSWERS.—Learned Hand
    Speech in New York City,
    Jan. 27, 1952.*

Part I

WHY TELL THIS NOW?

Is not this what I require of you as a fast:
to loose the fetters of injustice,
to untie the knots of the yolk,
to snap every yolk
and set free those who have been crushed?

—Isaiah 58:6–7

Chapter I

BY WAY OF INTRODUCTION

"Then you say that the auditor assigned the rental expenses for the posthole digger to the horses and other expenses of this particular section of the fencing to the cattle?"

No. Nothing to the cattle.

"Well, where did she itemize the many, many supplies you must have been buying?"

In a column on her exhibits labeled "Horses or Personal" or "All Others," whatever that might mean; I think she was trying to push all farming expenses onto either the horses or into an "indeterminate" column which she would later try to get me to agree should be prorated as to a cattle or pleasure category.

"What was this part of the fencing to be used for?"

An acre or so of woodland was being separated from the forest. It was close to the barn and was to be a sheltered area for the cattle during the winters. It was low land and therefore afforded a natural windbreak. There was a small creek running through it which rarely froze. This was important because I had not spent any money to have a well dug. The fencing served to keep the cows and calves out of the forest, the growth of which I was managing for long-term harvest. The horses have never been in it—nine years now. It would be a real hazard to an unmounted horse. I never saw a horse with cloven hooves.

"But Doctor, this is laughable."

It is now, but not at three o'clock each morning for six weeks while I was preparing my rebuttal for the third step up the IRS inquisitory ladder, the appellate conferee. But you may be right. *A laugh's the wisest, easiest answer to all that's queer.*[1]

"Why did you gather the arguments yourself?"

Well, I estimated the time it would take. I did it a little more rapidly than I figured, since when it is fired up, my mind functions pretty fast. *Depend upon it, Sir, when a man knows he is to be hanged in a fortnight, it concentrates his mind wonderfully.*[2] It took me close to 200 hours, with my spouse doing a lot of the leg work. Legal time in those days would have cost me about $10,000 and accountant fees might have been in the range of $6,000. Further, the two of them would just have slowed me down because they were not acquainted with every detail, and I would have had to teach them too much preliminarily. Besides, *the best way I know of to win an argument is to start by being in the right.*[3] I knew I was right and didn't want any legal or financial obfuscation.

"Could you tell me why you believe you were subjected to this type of harassment and then sort of start from a beginning point so that our readers will have the origin of this fight against the Internal Revenue Service?"

I will be glad to. The best reference I ran across to explain why I was picked for an audit can be found on page 1 of the *Wall Street Journal,* dated March 23, 1970. I have the clipping here for you but will read directly the sentences which I think are applicable. You later can see that I am not altering the context. The paper quotes one IRS official as stating that "the last thing we want to do is to put every tax cheat behind bars. The jails couldn't hold them all even if one could track them all down." Our Congress and the IRS do not realize that you and *I should never have known what it was to covet, if the law had not said, "Thou shalt not covet."*[4] The statement continues that they are "looking for cases with news potential—especially prized being those involving racketeers, corrupt public officials or pillars of the community like doctors or lawyers." The idea is expressed that through such a strategy "a few well-publicized convictions will strike terror in the hearts of the taxpayers wavering between honesty, evasion and taking a questionable deduction."

Contrarily, I think that most Americans feel it is *Better one hand full and peace of mind, than both fists full and toil that is chasing the wind.*[5] I sure had to toil against them with just one hand full.

Up to this point we could say, then, a physician with a farm which had a loss is a special prize—fair game for the IRS to hunt. Still, I was not in despair. Only in a sense did I wonder *Why hast thou made me thy butt/ and why have I become thy target?*[6]

A good place to begin is to indicate to you that when I first saw the audit and did a rapid calculation, the IRS was claiming that it cost us $7090.39 to feed and stable a child's pleasure horse for a year!

"You must have the decimal point in the wrong place."

No, I don't. Those were the disallowances for just the first of the three years undergoing audit at the same time.

"Those years were 1966, 1967, and 1968. Why not tell us why you have waited several years to tell us this story?"

First, the appellate conference was not held until 1970. Also, I suppose that like others I am a little lazy, but I learned from Ben Franklin that *laziness travels so slowly that poverty overtakes him,*[7] so I row a little faster than that. That's why we are writing this book. Besides, *Indolence is a delightful but distressing state; we must be doing something to be happy.*[8] It will make me happy to pay the IRS the taxes on the money I will gather into the second fist earned from this book. Also we are taught: *Don't yield to that alluring witch, Laziness, or else be prepared to surrender all that you have won in your better moments.*[9]

Another thing, it took me some time to unwind and get rid of excess adrenalin. You know the audit initiated the loss of one position that I held and enjoyed and to some extent I had to ready another life. Most of all, though, I am in another peculiar IRS spot and the continuing Revenue Service and congressional insanities bring it back strongly enough to mind to want to get it in print. Also, I have had a bad financial year—one of those in which factually you would have done better by not getting out of bed on January the first—and I want to recoup through the sale of these miserable experiences to your publishing house.

It is not a mystery to me that for about four months now I have been headed for another audit. Naturally, I am trying to avoid it. When I took on the last fight the amounts of money involved were quite enormous for a middle-income tax-bracket citizen. One had to fight. You know what General Ike said: *What counts is not necessarily the size of the dog in the fight—its the size of the fight in the dog.*[10] My interests back then were not as varied as now and there was a big kick gained from preparing the rebuttal. Now I don't want to waste the time. This time is not of a sort in which I would take my vacations on my neighbor's back porch or would remarry to get out of doing the dishes. I have won all my tax cases and would win again, but the time I am talking about is time to spend writing poetry, listening to good music, learning if anything is left of my singing voice so it can join in at piano bars, improving my teaching systems, polishing up my lectures, getting off the short-term investment gambles, and learning more about capital gains. In regard to the latter, if you can't beat the system, join it. Also, such concentrated effort to prove you are not a crook interferes with the enjoyment of life. There should be time to hunt and fish and to observe and participate in the third life. You have got to remember when you are fighting the IRS ghosts that you should try to *Never contend with a man who has nothing to lose.*[11]

Right now, at the end of this fiscal year, I am fencing against a double-edged saber.

"What do you mean by that term?"

One edge of the beheading, or more accurately, the castrating, device is that too much tax is being withheld from my salary. I am not alone in this. Newspapers are carrying the story today that $28,000,000,000 in federal tax refunds are waiting. How does the government know that? It isn't even December 31, no less next April 15! From their experience, that's how! This news release is talking about individual taxpayers, not corporations. A fair chunk of this is mine. It's my thinking that the greatest amount of this paltry 28 billion dollars is from salaried people, and the government has coerced us into giving them this interest-free money. The salaried person does not have the same advantages as does an independent contractor. Although *Every advantage has its tax,*[12] the independent soul can alter his quarterly returns so that by April Fool's Day he can come out about even. That is, his estimated tax for the fiscal year can be rearranged to come out close to reality—he would owe the feds little, or they would owe him little. There is a big advantage to this.

Do you know that there is no way that I could stop my major employer from withholding taxes for the remaining four months of this year? He might have done it but my tax consultant said, *"Nyet."* One could show some bare round figures to a third-grade oral arithmetician and he could easily figure that my taxes will have been overpaid (excess withheld) by many thousands of dollars by December 31.

"I am not sure I understand this and I passed the third grade."

It comes about this way: when you take a job, your employer gives you a piece of paper to sign on which you list your deductions. Then he uses a tax reference source which indicates how much he should withhold depending on numbers of kids and other minor items. This federal form assumes that you are a Middle Age peasant with no external financial interests or gambling instincts; that you are happy with the status quo of the paycheck. This system, if it is to be fair, must assume that you will never make more than $1,000 in stock transactions because although you have to pay taxes on all winnings in commodities, stocks, and the like, you cannot take deductions for losses greater than $1,000. The argument that a taxpayer can "carry over" losses greater than that amount to the following years falls in a decibel range my ears cannot hear, because my carryover from this year alone is so great that I will never be able to recoup if this body lasts to age eighty-nine. We all know that *When the age is in, the wit is out.*[13] If I die before that age, and thank goodness *Seventy years is the span of life/ eighty if our strength holds,*[14] I will never have had the solace of a tax reduction to compensate for the extremely poor judgment of my "expert" commodity representative. Age eighty-nine is my estimate of a few good years mixed in with this last real bad one, plus more to come, because this part-time entrepreneur does not expect ever to give up the excitement of investments.

Anyway, my stock losses are limited to $1,000 not by fact but by edict. Let's go on because this sum is a small portion of a big loss, not money-wise but tax-system-wise, and would not get me into an auditable stage by itself.

Seeing how bad the year was going to be and realizing that I was going to have to pay taxes on my salary although my true income was far less than the salary, I decided nevertheless to place venture capital in a gas and oil project which would reduce my taxes. I am a limited partner along with several others, who have joined with a general partner "to explore for, develop, produce and market gas and oil." As I get it from reading the prospectus and from smaller similar ventures my wife and I have participated in, existing statutory provisions of the Code permit the subtraction of intangible drilling expenses and other tax deductions such as wages, fuel, hauling, etc. in the year the expense was incurred. The general partner has indicated that he will push the drilling and it is expected that the greatest portion of the investment will be spent this year and that there will be no income since even if we hit gas there are no existing pipelines to transport it this year. Actually, we have hit both gas and oil and even though it is not marketable, the year is not as bleak as it otherwise looked except for a worsening audit aspect. You understand, do you not, that these further expenses increase the amount of money I will have to ask the IRS to return?

"I have never had the grand opportunity to ask the Revenue Service to return a lot of money to me. I have a lot of kids and could use it. What is so bad about that?"

About having a lot of kids?

"No, you know what I mean."

I'm getting to it.

I forgot to tell you that I am still a part-time farmer. Last year there were losses on the operation. I had bought calves for 58 cents a pound and sold them for 41 cents. These were originally 500-pounders which I just grassed out. My estimate was that I would gross close to $14,000 on them but when I bought them I did not of course know that our great congressional leaders would interfere with the supply-and-demand system of our "free" country. While their freeze on beef was in effect the price held up, but after September 12, 1973, when the freeze on prices was released, I sold the steers at a loss. The heifers no one wanted locally and they were finally shipped 800 miles to sell them. I did not want to wait until this year to sell since this would have meant a loss on this year's books, and as I will explain, the feds say I am to make a profit this year or incur their wrath by being challenged that I was running a hobby farm again.

After this 1973 debacle, and still being interested in cattle, I talked to my accountant and it was his opinion that if I did not operate a farm in 1974—just let it lie idle—I would not be filling out a farm IRS form for income-tax purposes and it could not be considered as a year in which I had to make a farm profit.

I decided to go this route and in February I bought a big herd—for me—of 50-cent yearlings but did not put them on my farm. A partnership was formed with a feeder and we put the cattle on his place. If the price went up to 60 cents by spring grazing time, as it did in 1973, we would make a handsome profit. Everyone wants steers in April. However, what with gas rationing, truck strikes, housewife boycotts, and the like, the value decreased by spring. But we had an alternative and we took it. We would hold them on his pastures with a light supplemental ration during the grass season and then would give them a hot ration during the fall and winter. This was a reasonable business concept since the fat cattle futures were sufficiently high then to allow us to make a buck. The characteristics of the partnership were: my cattle, his labor and buildings, share feed costs, share profits on gain in value of each steer.

This is not working either. The fat cattle market is very depressed and we did not hedge the animals, a very bad judgment. The reasons are complex but the major one is that the country has had a bad corn year and the price of corn makes it almost prohibitive to fatten cattle. Therefore, we are right now feeding them an intermediate ration and hoping that the price will increase in the new year enough to warrant feeding them to choice grade. Some restaurants are going to have to buy choice grade and the Cadillac owners will continue to buy choice meat.

The price presently is 28 cents. Remember, I paid 50 cents. Obviously, we will sell them next year. But watch this: calf costs are deducted in the year that you sell them, not the year that you buy. However, all the expenses—trucking, silage, grain, fertilizer for pasture, equipment repair, and depreciation—are deducted in the year they occurred, or more properly, were paid. If I sold them this year, my losses would be astronomical. But without selling them, the only losses are the running expenses.

"Why don't you just fill out a form W-4 for your employer and have done with it?"

Well I see you came prepared for this session, but you are wrong. That form is for more kids, more minor contributions, interest payments. Who knows why it is not for business losses?

Anyway, money—not taxes—continue to get deducted from my good-sized paycheck. Let me point out the consequences. The federal government this minute has too much of my income and it is not taxable; all the excess belongs to me, not to them. They are investing it, if not wasting it along with the rest of that $28,000,000,000, and gaining interest. They should be paying us interest. If my share were in my bank, the interest would be making a bad year for many of us a little better. Further, most Americans are having a cash-flow problem; me, too. You have to sell this or that or exchange that for this to relieve the problem. For instance, my wife Sarah and I had the best nontaxable bond we ever owned but exchanged its money value for the gas-and-oil investment because our cash flow was not big enough for that amount which was necessary to hold them both, the feds holding my money, illegally, in my opinion; the legality I am not going to expound on but leave that to previously published books.

These two particulars do not bother me excessively since

I can live with them. I can live with sin. They cause mostly a screaming resentment but not a murderous one. The sin and murder are something like this. *Madigan and O'Skelley were being sentenced for murder. "Do you have anything to say?" asked the judge. "I'm sorry they caught us!" said Madigan. "Then you confess now that you killed the man." "We might've done it," said O'Skelley, "if it don't do no harm to say so now." "How did you do it?" the judge inquired. "I struck him with a stone," answered Madigan. "And O'Skelley hit him with a shillelagh and then we buried him." "What did you do before you buried him?" "We searched him!" said O'Skelley. "And what did you find?" "Two dollars and a roast beef sandwich." replied Madigan. "You kept the money, I'm sure, but what did you do with the sandwich?" "We was hungry," said O'Skelley, "so we ate the bread and threw away the meat." "Why'd you throw away the roast beef?" "Your honor," said Madigan, "It was Friday. It'd been a sin to eat the meat!"*[15]

Besides, whom was I going to murder? *What can you do by killing? Nothing. You kill one dog, the master buys another—that's all there is to it.*[16]

However, what bugs me, and we now get back both to the third-grader and the first cutting edge of the saber, the size of the overpayment alone is likely to be high enough to trigger an IRS computer to earmark my return for another audit.

Overpayment!! What an invented term; only the IRS could insult us so neatly. It sounds like we peons have so much money lying under the straw mattress that we prefer to give them more than our accounting and have them care for it. It is not an overpayment. It is a deliberate overdeduction.

The computer, then, we having been cheated by overdeductions, a real theft, is programmed to sniff this out like a dog programmed to sniff out opium, as a highly likely suspicious tax return. Can you beat that?

"But, Dr. Whitely, you have not done anything dishonest. You have just made bad investments. An honest man should not fear an audit."

You must have been brought up in a monastery. The national theme is that an accuser has to prove you are dishonest by trial by jury. The IRS is not in the national flow. You are automatically considered to be a crook. You have to prove that you are honest, and this takes time, as you will soon hear. And there is more to it than the money. *Who steals my purse steals trash; 'tis something, nothing/ 'Twas mine, 'tis his, and has been slave to thousands./ But he that filches from me my good name/ Robs me of that which not enriches him/ And makes me poor indeed.*[17]

I have some other losses, some deductible, some not, the former increasing the amount of the stolen money returnable to me.

"What is the second edge of their fencing saber?"

You know, maybe when we write this in final form, I should not use the term. The present saber is for sport; on the other hand, maybe a double-edged one is not. I'm vacillating here, like the IRS, because hunting is a sport and that is really what the IRS does.

The second edge is honed by my farm. There is just one remaining now. The other two were sold because they were in a distant state and because I couldn't refuse the good offers made for them. There was no kick left in just owning them and not operating them. The profit was a capital-gains one and the sales gave me some cash that could be used nearer my present home.

Recently the rules have changed about farms. It is not a change in an IRS regulation but a law promulgated by Congress. This is why *It is no good dreaming dreams of utopia if one cannot draft the appropriate legislation.*[18] Presently, a farm has to show a profit for two out of every five years; otherwise shoveling cow manure is a hobby. It used to be one out of each five years. This funny law turns out to be retroactive. Since I made a profit in 1972, I had figured that the next *profit requirement* in this *free country* would be

1976; not so according to my accountant's interpretation of this congressional action. Without going into the detail, I must make a profit this year.

Please ask me what Will Rogers, Mark Twain, and others have said about Congress.

"O.K., I'm asking."

"*A Congressman is never any better than his roads, and sometimes worse.*"[19]

"*It could probably be shown by facts and figures that there is no distinctly native American criminal class except Congress.*"[20]

And last, even though I am enjoying this: "*Congress—these, for the most part, illiterate hacks whose fancy vests are spotted with gravy, and whose speeches, hypocritical, unctious, and slovenly are spotted also with the gravy of political patronage.*"[21]

I have explained the farm loss for 1973. This year the situation is even worse. You recall me telling you that I had decided not to operate the farm. However, the price of weaned calves had not risen from the time I bought the speculative herd in February. Also, the feeder cattle futures projected for fall were real great. With these things in mind and a wet spring pushing my pastures into lovable lushness, the world starving, population soaring abroad, increasing numbers of bleeding hearts, meat consumption per capita in the States rising, I decided to go the business route again. What would you do with all that grass? Also being a biologist, I wanted to experiment with fighting pinkeye which over the years had reduced weight gains, increased my workload, and blinded my bulls. I wanted to get rid of this infectious monstrosity. I wasn't any more sure that it could be licked than I was sure what type of Russian roulette Congress would hatch up in 1974; so I hedged the herd, not on the commodity market, but by plowing up one of the poorer pastures and having it planted in corn.

My analysis of the situation, mostly based on futures markets for corn and feeder cattle, was that the farm would gross about $12,000 above the cost of the calves and cost of getting the corn harvested. My other expenses—depreciation, fuel, repairs, and minimal outside labor—are very modest, and there was plenty room left for feeding the herd liquid nitrogen and a little cracked corn for better daily gain. Well, my great success was in containing pinkeye; that's all that was accomplished. The 50-cent calves are worth 28 cents, like the partnership herd. The corn which we expected to gather in November is still standing in fields too wet to work.

So here we taxpayers are at year and wits' end, trying to outsmart a computer. If the cattle are sold this year, we cannot avoid the IRS guillotine. But if they are sold next year, I do not have to expense their basic cost until then. How do I make a profit for Schedule F, the farm schedule? I really cannot easily but if a way can be found for someone to buy the corn standing in the field, it will help. Now, to make up the difference.

The only thing to do is to sell timber from my forests. This is not a very good business objective, since timber value is depressed with the absence of new housing starts and the resultant absence of a good furniture market.

Believe it or not, I managed to do both and the checks are in the bank. I will pay a few bills, but not all, on December 31, making sure that there is some tax to pay (it turned out to be $83.00), leaving the rest of the expenses till next year, a somehow magical one in which I don't have to make a profit.

Aren't these financial gyrations silly for an American? Of course, I could give up the practice of medicine. This would make me a "full-time" farmer on the same small piece of land and it could no longer be attacked as a hobby!

Imagine how I felt when this morning after all this devious but legal thinking and doing to get this accomplished, I read how our congressman in his *Washington Report* is going to settle the country's financial woes. Remember, he represents me. After an introduction attesting to the paramount problems, as well known to most of us as to him, he lists his economic policy. These are itemized. After cautiously stating as Item I that the Federal Reserve System should ease credits with buts, he follows with Item II advocating that the system should "channel" credit to the productive segments such as agriculture. However, his Item IIIa calls for a comprehensive tax reform package, listing just five, and what do you think one of the five is? Yes, the elimination of hobby-farm tax deductions. *Their speech is smoother than butter.*[22]

In the last eleven years, I have been all over this county, which is the largest in his district, first looking for a farm on which one could make an honest dollar and then buying and operating one part-time. I cannot find a hobby farm. Picking up grain recently (which cost me 6.35 cents a pound to feed to these calves now that the pasture is gone) at a large local market I asked two knowledgeable people where there is a hobby farm in this county. Neither knew of one. I suppose the congressman would say his district is pure. The hobby farms are elsewhere.

Actually, for many years a farm owner did not have to raise a single crop to be a success; that is, he would let the land lie idle, go to the local office of the Agricultural Stabilization and Conservation Service, sign some papers, and pick up a handsome check later for having the land stand in the "soil bank." How would you like to be in a no-risk business, and a nonhobby one at that? The IRS could not attack that; no way. In our county, the names of the major recipients of this largess are published and there are more major-time farmers collecting this type of green crop than part-time owners. This past pathetic congressional pet is one of the reasons grain and red meat products have been so high in cost. If you are a cattleman you need cheap land to hold down costs. One could not readily buy this land because the manna from Washington exceeded each year the amount in interest that banks would pay on the money the landowner would get for selling properly priced pastureland. Why should he sell? He was making more money by "banking" the land instead of money and he still owned the land. The artificial prices for the poorer pastureland in turn threw up the price for land suitable for grain production.

Just as from a realistic business standpoint, rather than from an enforced one, I do not care to sell timber now, I do not want to sell my corn now. Corn is still being harvested, and there is lots of it for sale. I want to hold it for a better price. Corn trucks have been standing in line overnight waiting to weigh in at local scales.

I want to keep my corn either for the better price or to help feed my several loads of steers. You recall the price to me for buying it is 6.35 cents a pound. Anticipating 100 bushels to the acre, my corn has cost me just 0.86 cents plus tax on the land out of pocket. (To would-be farmers, I suggest they add the interest on the land investment.)

Imagine the marbling I could get into cattle with corn costing about a penny a pound. Aren't you drooling over the taste the steaks would have? My farm, by early next year, would show a great profit from the weight gains on this cheap feed. It would entice me to expand. The more nuts like me who discount the present value of the land and who expand, the less the meat costs you. If I didn't want to sell this book to you, I would say go get some new store-bought teeth to use to chew up the "fat" cattle meat you will soon be buying from steers slaughtered right off grass or silage.

Tell me, isn't this a crummy way for a taxpayer to conduct a legitimate business? He is forced onto nonsensical paths. On a two-year basis I could make a good profit.

Well, anyway, the dollar-plus profit I have "arranged" for my farm will dull one edge of the saber.

I just decided I will not pay a $3,457.70 invoice for my share of corn I bought for the off-farm cattle partnership this year either. Maybe that will lower the amount of tax refund the IRS will have to give me to a dollar figure below the trigger point for the computer.

This may not have answered your question about why I

have waited several years to tell the story about the $7,090.39 feed bill for a child's pet, but does it explain why I want to tell the story now?

"Yes, it does."

Do you have any more questions, or can I go ahead and tell the big story uninterrupted. I am not in a big hurry like my neighbor whom I saw pushing his car to work so he would not have to waste time getting into it.

"One more question. There must be other books written for lay people on income tax. Why do you want to publish?"

Yes, indeed, other books have been written. Those I have read are mostly in generalities although specific instances are used to make up the generality. Some point out that the federal income tax is unconstitutional and that people should know about these illegalities and resist them through reaction, including not submitting a Form 1040. You can read about alternatives by which the money needed to run the government can be raised without interfering so much with our lives. It is even pointed out that taxation is a form of theft and that it can be deduced logically that therefore taxation is an immorality. *Why is it that your master eats with tax-gatherers and sinners? Jesus heard it and said "It is not the healthy that need a Doctor but the sick."*[23]

One author feels that the IRS is a conspiracy to lead to totalitarianism. A text is available in which the reader gets an inside view of the workings of the mind of an IRS auditor with an advocacy of the proper psychological approaches.

Pamphlets can be purchased or drawn from public libraries that indicate that the tax is a fraud milking the wage earner and rewarding the rich. You will find that taxpayers have been able to complain before committees of the U.S. Senate and that stories of these episodes can be found in national magazines.

My interests are not in these directions, although the data are useful and very revealing. It is clear to me that the major job of the federal government is to secure our mutual defense. This takes a lot of money. I want my government to have all the money its experts judge is needed for this terribly difficult task. Its job is hard since we compete with slave labor. *There is a sufficiency in the world for man's need but not for man's greed.*[24]

The morality or legality of the *entire* system, although of concern to me, is not my present task. *The devil can cite Scripture for his purposes.*[25] If there be illegalities let us correct them but let us be taxed. *No morality can be founded on authority, even if the authority were divine.*[26]

I want to write a spoof. I want to show incompetence, not necessarily due to inherent incapacity, although I think this exists, or to inherent nonintelligence of an agent, but that incapacity of undertraining or the incompetence due to nonclarity of promulgations. I want to stress that agents should be culpable for their actions and poor judgments. I want to plead that there be continuity in the thesis of taxation, that the directives and regulations be as clear to a taxpayer as they should be from one auditor to the next; that you cannot write in the smokestack with black crayon. I want that less judgment be required from the auditor; that guidelines be sharper. I want to demonstrate by my experiences that without an adequacy of knowledge the agents can become—do become—agents of harassment—that this should not be allowed; that agents should be required to appear as witnesses in their own behalf and on behalf of the taxpayer just as are arresting police officers; that they can find themselves placed in a position of perjury just as we are.

The IRS seems to become a religion to some agents. *Men never do evil so completely and cheerfully as when they do it from religious conviction.*[27]

I long for a system which is not a ridiculous one. There should be recourses for injustices to the honest taxpayer. I am not talking about who finally may or may not win—money—in a tax court.

We will be talking about percentages. How far wrong may an agent be? Should he be able to audit a taxpayer and be thousands of percentage points off from what the taxpayer has claimed? It seems that *A learned blockhead is a greater blockhead than an ignorant one.*[28] How can it be that an auditor and a regional conferee (next step up the ladder) can be in absolute concurrence down to a penny as to the taxpayer's unjust debt, but by going one step higher in the conference procedure, the next human being finds the presumed debt unjust? Is he better trained? Is he more compassionate? Is he wiser? Do the uses of staples and labor and do the uses of pesticide sprays change between two rungs in the same ladder? Some of the features are as insensible as in this story. *Weinberg came home unexpectedly and found Mrs. Weinberg in bed with another man. "What the hell are you doing?" shouted the irate husband. "See?" said his wife to the man beside her, "Didn't I tell you he was stupid?"*[29]

I can recognize that there might be dispute about how much gasoline might be illegally or inadvertently used by the taxpayer for personal versus business driving. What I can not recognize is the stupidity of declaring legitimate expenses improper and by adding these up one on top of the other *ad infinitum* so that the differences in the dispute are not a matter of a few percentage points but hundreds or thousands of percentage points. I can understand how it could be challenged that a fourth of a mile of fencing was for personal use but how can it be argued that nearly 100 percent is for pleasure use on a cattle farm?

I think arbitration with an IRS official should be on a relatively high level. The way it ran was more like this conversation between two friends: *Sokolow: "I just got a beautiful French poodle for my wife." Newman: "Tell me, how did you get such a good trade?"*[30]

I can even understand that the nature of a business can change from one tax year to another so that an agent should challenge a depreciation schedule where it is evidently no longer appropriate. However, if the agent can change his opinion about uses just arbitrarily, then the honest taxpayer has no hope for the future of his business.

Further, it is my intent, useless perhaps, to cry out to

show the IRS folk that they are wrong, to try to have them mend, knowing full well that *A thousand curses never tore a sheet.*[31] I do not want to keep my mouth closed. Generally I am pretty quiet and don't open it much. In fact, once I went out to fetch the morning paper while I was wearing leather-bottom slippers. The grass the newspaper was on was still wet with dew. I took the paper in one hand and a glass of cola in the other and started down the stairs to my basement office. I slipped, landing on the bottom with a dislocated shoulder. I managed to get to the phone and called a neighbor for help. When he arrived and saw the spilled drink he accused me of waiting to call him until I swallowed the hootch in my mouth.

It is my philosophy to be one of those who feel *We shall repent in this generation, not so much for the evil deeds of the wicked people, but for the appalling silence of the good people.*[32] You will read in the Bible to *Never remain silent when a word might put things right.*[33]

There is no reason that the objectives of the audit not be clear to both parties. If they had been as clear on day one as I wrote them on day 431 for the appellate conferee, the entire matter lended itself to early settlement. All audits can be divided into arithmetic areas and contestable areas. The first bows to simple mathematics. The contested areas must be very clear and *definable on paper,* and most should be amenable to settlement by clearly defined guidelines. The minimal remainder should be settled by disinterested experts engaged by both parties.

It is my hope that by using ridicule as a weapon, and by communicating mockery, that the ridiculous can be stopped. *The most effective way of attacking vice is to expose it to public ridicule. People can put up with rebukes but they cannot bear to be laughed at. They are prepared to be wicked but they dislike appearing ridiculous.*[34]

Can I make this more succinct? When the final conference was completed I asked the appellate officer what he had learned. I was not being a wiseguy. The question was without subtlety of any kind—just forthright. There was no sneer in my voice. I truly wanted to know the impact of my long and tough task. He said that he had learned. And I asked what he intended to do with this new understanding. His reply was as humble as my question—that he could do nothing, that the organization was too vast, that his role was too small. Just like one of us then, his voice is too small.

But what about many of us? *Let us remember, when we are inclined to be disheartened that the private soldier is a poor judge of the fortunes of a great battle.*[35]

What follows makes public what was essentially private. Let others learn about one's success so that more will have a trail to guide them and that more will join against this religion of tyranny.

To you honest subscribers to this labor, learn how to fight ludicrous audits. The bugle call has to be very clear, so that you will be prepared to battle. *Those who go to war should fight to achieve some good or avoid some evil.*[36]

Know what your final statements will be. Everything must lead to them. They are the peak of your pyramid. All the blocks leading to them must be sound.

Get down on paper every word coming from the mouths of the agents. Fight each positive statement made by them on paper with contrary and superior statements by experts among your friends or business associates. They have more combined knowledge than can possibly one or two auditors. The agents are slippery and since you cannot yet get an affidavit from them or about them from their superiors, then recall statements they have made from your own notes. Place yourself in jeopardy from perjury by attesting to their statements. It is easy. *There are not fifty ways of fighting, there is only one: To be the conquerer.*[37]

Immediately after the final conference, a federal lawyer who had been sitting in on the procedures followed me to the johnny and above the streams said, "Doctor, that was the finest rebuttal I have ever read or heard."

Some months after I thought it was all over, I met Mr.

Cicada of the IRS, who will be introduced to you in the next chapter, and he asked if anyone had told me of any follow-up. It turned out that the lowest-echelon groups of the IRS can challenge the decision of the upper echelon, that this was done by auditor Blondie N. Olittle, and that the Sultan of the district himself said, in effect, get off the doctor's back.

How lovely on the mountains are the feet of the herald who came to proclaim prosperity and bring good news, the news of deliverance.[38]

Well, that is the end of the beginning.

"Go ahead now with your verbatim arguments as you wrote them to the appellate conferee."

O.K. I will change from time to time from "I" to "we" since the returns are joint and the IRS considers my wife an accomplice in crime. Please remember that we are writing not of misunderstandings between us and federal auditors but of alterations in my books that they were trying to effect. There is a big difference.

"Oh, my darling," the middle aged lover said to his Polish girl friend. "I want you for my wife." Indignantly, the Polish chick said, "I don't know as I like that. I much prefer men."[39]

I bought my first farm in 1961; by no coincidence, regardless of IRS assertions, I soon had my first audit.

Part II

THE ARGUMENT

Somebody has to have the last word.
If not, every argument could be opposed
by another and we'd never be done with it.
                    —*Albert Camus,* The Fall

Chapter II

A THESIS

The Fifth Freedom, The Freedom of Individual Enterprise is the Keystone of the Arch on which the other Four Freedoms Rest.[1]

For consideration by: Mr. John B. Nice
                                      Appellate Conferee
                                      Internal Revenue Service
                                      Midtown, Midamerica

Prepared by: Roger Whitely, M.D.
                                        Sarah Whitely

Reasons: A conference was requested of you since the taxpayers do not accept:

    a. Audits of 1966, 1967, and 1968 by Mrs. Blondie N. Olittle
    b. Conference considerations, same years, by Mr. I.M. Crackpot.

Section I. Arguments concerning IRS statements about our farm businesses

Rights: All rights are reserved in regard to this section; no part of this section may be reproduced in any form, handwritten, typed, copied by copy-machine, taped, photographed, used for television or radio without the express permission, in writing, from Roger Whitely, M.D.

The sheet of paper I have just handed to you is the first page of the opus I wrote in argument against the auditor and her regional conferee concerning my tax returns for three years. It was to the appellate conferee. Such conference is the third step up the IRS ladder. The taxpayer is allowed to present his material in argumentative form. When you publish this, please print all material that I sent him in different typeset or indent it and also treat my letters sent to IRS persons preliminarily in the same fashion. This should help the readers to distinguish the submitted data from verbiage such as this. My product was 101 pages long, including affidavits and references. It could have been longer but I didn't want something like this to happen: *There was the Polack farmer who wrote a Chicago mail order house asking for their special rate on toilet paper. The mail order clerk, in his letter of reply, told the Polack to consult page 27 of the company's catalogue. To which the Polack wrote back with some irritation, "Listen, dummy, if I had your catalogue, you think I'd need toilet paper?"*[2]

I decided to put my arguments in writing because if they got nowhere with him, then the material would act as the context of a legal brief if we had to proceed to the fourth rung which is the tax court. There was no intention on my part to have to rework oral material into written material for the court action.

There can be multiple approaches to any problem. I selected a course which would indicate that the IRS was a destructive agency; that it had incompetents within it; that the agents were inconsistent from agent to agent and from year to year; that their activities were offensive, insensitive, and harassing; that they should be made accountable if not suable.

My third decision was to challenge any specific written statement by the auditor by means of an affidavit from someone more knowledgeable than she. The response to this latter was exciting and very productive. As we proceed, you

will find affidavits not only from friends and associates but
from other agencies or employees of the federal government!

That first line heading up the text is used for my thesis;
it is a statement by Nicholas Murray Butler, noted author
and educator, not my own. He is saying that the freedom of
individual enterprise follows in importance, but indeed
shoulders the first four freedoms of speech, religion, press,
and of congregation.

Let us go back to your question of why I waited so long
to let the public read this story. You will notice from the
material at the bottom of the page that at that time, which
was the spring of 1970, I must have had in mind the publication of this material. I warned the Revenue Service in the
sentence on "rights" not to reproduce any of it without my
permission (author's rights).

My next two pages I put in the form of a prologue, and
I'll wait a minute here to give you time to read it.

ARGUMENTS CONCERNING INTERNAL REVENUE
SERVICE
STATEMENTS ABOUT OUR FARM BUSINESSES

PROLOGUE

Sir:

Besides being a physician underpaid for my out-
standing managerial and administrative skills in non-
professional matters, I have been and am a successful
operator and owner of combined timber and cow-calf operations. I have been in this type of business since
1961, both in a southern commonwealth and the state
of Midamerica. I will subsequently refer you to two
segments of material signed by me under penalty of
perjury and recently forwarded to a division of the U.S.
government, attesting this success.

In the instance of both of these crops, not one crop

as falsely indicated by the auditor, it is noteworthy that profit is not realized in the first tax year, as it is in the practice of medicine and in salaried positions. Nevertheless, you will find as the thesis progresses that time and study have their rewards, as does patience and perseverance, and knowhow. For 1969, I am paying the federal government taxes on $13,249 profit on these separated farm businesses. The taxes on this $13,249 will go a long way in providing my country with money to provide for our security and to promote (overpromote) our welfare as well as to aid with unnecessary expenditures.

I could and probably should end my argument here since it already refutes the absolutely astounding claims of the auditor and her concurring conferee, but since 1969 is not yet a year under audit, I shall proceed. However, since 1969 *will* be audited and since it has significant bearing on some of the audited years' remarks, I shall also proceed. Further, since there are monies owed me by my country, which I had not previously bothered with, but which I now intend to collect, since the IRS has made a big issue out of a small one just as it did in 1964 and was 2,700 percent wrong and in 1965 when it was 1,600 percent wrong. Also there are three points in regard to my Midamerica farm that I want settled. I do not say "settled for once and for all" because my thesis will show you that the inconsistencies of the IRS from year to year do not permit such a sensible statement.

You probably have been reading of the U.S. Department of Agriculture tests on bologna and its declaration that bologna has 49.6 percent water content. This department, with one employee for about every twenty farmers, failed to indicate a reasonably similar content in steaks. Considering the number of IRS personnel involved in farms, the federal employee-to-farmer ratio is even higher.

Do you find fear in this? *Fear is nothing but the abandonment of the aid that comes from reason.*[3] Actually, the inferences are several. If I have been operating pleasure farms why am I paying taxes on profit in 1969? From where did the profits derive? Are pleasures taxable now? You will note that in 1964, the auditor was wrong about my tax return, not in an amount of 2.7 percent, which I could forgive as a reasonable biological (man) error, not in the amount of 27 percent, which could still be a feasible, but honest error on my part or the auditor's part. He was wrong not to an extent of 270 percent which should put me in a criminal class, but he was wrong as much as 2,700 percent! Yet, you will see later a declaration by the IRS that its auditors are well trained and competent. What physical or biological or financial or cultural system can survive if it is 2,700 percent wrong? Only the IRS. You and I and the IRS know that *"Truth stumbles in the market place"*[4] but which untruthful taxpayer would take a chance to be a 2,700 percent liar?

The prologue also implies that the IRS is full of bologna. It turns out also that the one to twenty ratio of federal employees to farmers is increased not only by the interminably incorrect meddling of the agents of another branch of the government, the revenue group, which the agricultural department does not count, because they do not appear on their budget sheets, but now the Bureau of Census is in the act in an expensive way. I know; I have just filled out a questionnaire several score pages long which had 38 different sections to it.

The emotion, then, is not one of fear but of disgust and a need to lampoon while striking back.

Chapter III

THE BEGINNING OF THE STORY

The story starts in early February, 1969. At this time the term "Ms" had not caught on and I received a telephone call from a "person" using a female first name but no Miss or Mrs. She advised me that I was to undergo another audit. I had just finished one a few months previously which had dragged out for 17 months and had resulted in the national government wasting its time and your money.

I recollect being polite. During the brief conversation in which she was attempting to set up a meeting date to audit the 1966 and 1967 tax returns, she made a very obvious mistake, so I hedged a bit while one part of my mind was mouthing words and the other part thinking ahead. The auditor had just said that I had sold a farm in 1967. There had been no such sale. How wrong can an auditor get to be? There was nothing in my tax return to indicate there was such a sale. Was she accusing me of falsifying my return and pocketing the money from the sale without showing a tax liability? my mind was thinking. Was she just a "Blondie," or a nut, or a mistake-prone person?

It was already evident to me that the auditor who had been selected would foul up further if we proceeded with a series of meetings and that a portion of my time would have to be used in teaching her just as I had had to teach previous auditors such things as that cows were not placed on this green earth on the same day and therefore would differ in productive life and depreciation scheduling, and that standing timber on God's little acres, when cut, is a capital item if owned over six months. How would you like to deal with such "well-trained" people year after year?

The conversation concluded without an appointment. I used some excuse that eludes my memory. However, I immediately wrote a representative in the local Revenue Service office. This agent was generally recognized in the community as being "boss" of the outfit. It turns out that the "heads" of such offices are not the heads. There is always a "supervisor" in the bush. Anyway, my letter to him mentioned the .000 batting average of the Ms who in my letter I referred to as Miss/Mrs. since I don't think it polite to start off a letter to a woman with her first name, unless she is known to you personally.

Do you like the informality of this first contact? Notice, please, I have no letter to even indicate the spellings of her names. Nor did I early ever see a letter from her over signature. This phone contact rather than letter contact is deliberate as our readers will get to learn.

The conversation reminded me of a 1940 message by telephone from First Army Headquarters telling me that, as a reservist, I was called to active duty and to start packing. I told that officer-clerk that I do not acknowledge telephone calls as an order to military duty and that he should cut some orders (which he did).

Don't you think there should be a little more grace and formality for world wars and tax wars?

I include the entire letter. This way you will get to know me better.

5000 15th Street
Pomona, Midamerica
Feb. 9, 1969

Mr. Joseph Cicada
Internal Revenue Service
927 Versailles St.
Pomona, Midamerica.

Dear Mr. Cicada:

Miss or Mrs. Blondie N. Olittle has advised me that I am to undergo *another* tax audit. This is written since I am unable to reach you by phone.

I have several inquiries:

(1) Why am I selected for such frequent audits? (1963) (1964–1965) (1966–1967)?

(2) How is it that some physicians in this community, on the other hand have never had audits and others with much less frequency?

Since undoubtedly, your reflections on the above responses will not cancel the inspection, I include the following:

(1) The Federal Government has lost money on the previous audits.

(2) It will lose money on the coming 1966-1967 audits.

(3) Miss or Mrs. N. Olittle is already batting .000 on telephone conversation (i.e. "you sold a farm in 1967"—I sold no farm).

(4) I do not care to have anyone as an inspector of my tax returns who has had less than 5 years experience in this work with citizens in *my income category,* with one exception.

(5) Although Mr. B. Rong's experience is less than 5 years, he knows me and my account books and businesses and we have been through the fires sufficiently together so this should not drag out for another 17 months as did the last and which I considered an imposition on my time and equanimity.

(6) If you persist in selecting Miss or Mrs. N.

Olittle, I will automatically ask for a conferee of the astute and knowledgeable character of Mr. I.M. Crackpot, for anything other than arithmetic mistakes if her experience is less than five years.

(7) With Mr. Rong I will not automatically ask for a conference but will decide this after reasonable discussion with him.

(8) However, I then assume that Mr. Rong has received the proper technical advice relating to my previous returns as has Mr. Crackpot and has Mr. Charlie Comlately (Midtown) from the national office per letter 430, March 18, 1968.

In consideration of your response, I am

Very truly yours,
Roger Whitely, M.D.

The questions were entirely rhetorical. You know this; I know it and I am sure the senior local agent or whatever-name-anyone-can-find-for-him knew it. However, I wanted to get in some licks early and I wanted some things on paper for future use.

The physicians I knew to have had audits were those with farm businesses. I knew their problems and was staying away from exotic $3,000 cows and fancy $8,000 bulls. My farm was not being run for depreciation purposes and for a sellout in five years for capital gains and reduced taxes. Some cattle were purebred but commercial without pedigree papers.

Parenthetically note that my statement in the second item (2) was a true prediction.

I had decided that I was going to be adamant about item (6).

The response to this was quite rapid but very indirect. A letter arrived from someone calling himself a group supervisor. The letterhead was from the district director's office, which was a fabrication because I ultimately forced this ghost to give me his actual business address. The local agent never responded but just shifted. I don't think any of the questions were too hard even for a local yokel. I don't see anything in the response from the "supervisor" that his junior should not have known. Do they keep secrets from each other? Don't they train each other? Do they not share experiences? I don't think of them as free agents.

Anyway, I finally had a letter in file which I could beat at if needed. I am convinced that their aversion to letters is that a taxpayer can reproduce the letter or even use it in a legal brief, but cannot reproduce a telephone conversation. However, later you will learn how to reproduce IRS mouthings.

But were you to examine the original letter you would find no street address. Actually even the district director does not have an address other than the name of a large city! I suppose to get it you could travel to the city and get out a Ma Bell directory then travel back to your town with the address to get off a registered letter. Are they in hiding from the wrath of the public? Legal advisors indicate that I must exclude addresses, even fictitious ones as well as fictitious signatures for the six letters from the IRS in this novel and that precise dates should not be given.

U.S. Treasury Department
Internal Revenue Service
District Director
A City, USA.
Early 1969

Roger Whitely, M.D.
5000 15th Street
Pomona, Midamerica

Dear Dr. Whitely:

Your letter dated February 9, 1969 to Mr. Joseph Cicada of our Pomona office has been referred to the undersigned for reply. I will attempt to answer your questions in the order in which they were presented. First, as to why your return was selected for examination. The number of times a taxpayer has been examined in the past has nothing to do with the selection of a return. There are many taxpayers whose returns have been examined every year for ten or twenty years. Returns are now selected electronically for possible examination and are subjected to further screening by classifiers whose job it is to determine whether the errors and issues, both apparent and potential, warrant further examination. In your case, the fact that the issue in controversy in the prior examination was settled in District Conference, does not preclude further consideration of this issue in future years.

Second, why other physicians have had no audits or much fewer: The Internal Revenue Service does not conduct mass audits of taxpayers in particular professions or occupations. The returns are selected according to the procedures stated above.

Third, your concern as to the experience of the examining agent: I can appreciate your feeling that the agent should be competent and experienced and I can further assure you that Mrs. N. Olittle is a very competent examiner. The Internal Revenue Service sets very high standards for the selection of its agents and they receive intensive training after they are selected both in classroom courses and on-the-job training.

Fourth, your reference to Mr. Rong: It is not possible for Mr. Rong to perform this examination since the service has a policy that no examiner may follow himself on an examination, except in very large and complicated cases where considerable time may be saved by using the same examiner. An example of this would be a very large corporation with many subsidiaries.

I realize that an income tax examination can be very disturbing to a busy man but I am sure that if you make pertinent records available to Mrs. N. Olittle, the examination can be concluded with as little disturbance as possible to your schedule.

Sincerely yours,
Signature
Group Supervisor

What does this communication say?

If the number of times a taxpayer has been examined in the past has nothing to do with the selection of a return, the agency must be incompetent. If a taxpayer has been cheating in the past, do you not think that his returns should be automatically earmarked to be sure he has been straightened out? I read in this same paragraph that since there was a controversy about a part of a previous 1040 (nonfarm) of mine and they lost at the national level (not district conference level) they would take another crack at me. And they did on this same issue and this time refused to send the question back to Washington or to accept Washington's previous decision!

His second paragraph we have already batted down with the article you have from the *Wall Street Journal.*

The third paragraph—well, you will judge for yourself, the competence of this auditor. His "very competent examiner" was off in my presumed delinquency by 1,190 percent in 1966, 718 percent in 1967 and 2,786 percent in 1968! Again to emphasize the magnitude of her error and that I am not putting decimals in the wrong places: not 2.7 percent or 27.8 percent or 278.6 percent, but by thousands of percentages. *They boast of their wisdom, but they make fools of themselves.*[1]

The fourth paragraph must be considered a description of a stupid policy. I say stupid to contrast with sensible. The only sensible reason that an examiner should not follow himself would be that he is not to be trusted—that he is corruptible. It is seemingly all right, though, if he takes graft from a "very large corporation with many subsidiaries." *A clever man conceals his knowledge, but a stupid man broadcasts his folly.*[2]

The fifth paragraph gives no cognizance to the 17 months of disturbance from the previous audit.

It would have been foolhardy for me not to acknowledge to myself that I was stuck with an immature auditor. There was no sense in pursuing this path. It was apparent already that their feathers were ruffled since their iron curtain was protecting their auditor. The proof of this comes soon in the guise of a 6-foot-4 guy.

Obediently but reluctantly I wrote the Ms; but I still did

not set up an appointment. I decided to take high ground with my back to the sun; I would use my gun, item 6, letter of February 9, at which time I had just patted its holster. She was to prepare four separate lists for me, before I would meet with her: one each of arithmetic errors she found in each of the two years; and one each of other inquiries for each year. The interview, if I received these lists, would be conducted in my home study, not her office, and that I would contact her as to the time.

For reasons unknown to me, I received no reply for four months. Maybe she was boning up on farms. At long last she came up with a letter claiming she had found two (small) errors in 1966, none in 1967, and now since another April 15 had come and gone, she would also inspect the 1968 return! Perhaps they were waiting for this purpose. This letter, the first from the auditor, had no address on it nor did the envelope.

Finally, we got together.

Let us remember that an auditor is supposed to take the position of an independent third party and is to be the arbitrator between the taxpayer and the government and equally to protect our interests.

As she came through the door, I asked her if she was a Miss or Mrs., which almost knocked my spouse off her feet because she saw before I (I always look at a woman's face first) that the Ms was pregnant. All I learned about the male companion was that he was big, not the husband, and belonged to the ghost group. He surely was not there to hold her coat, since I was not going to physically battle her. I was not even going to bother with her, nor him. He was there to hold her arm. Apparently, the group supervisor must have lost some of his confidence over the intervening months, whereas previously he had given us his assurance that she was a very competent examiner, you recall.

This meeting did not last very long. I let her start. She did this by saying rigidly, "I will not allow you more than 50 percent on your farm truck." Some arbitration. Some third party. I should have been overjoyed, though. At least she acknowledged that I had a farm. But, before I forget, let me say here that on her ultimate figures she didn't even allow 50 percent. I guess she got madder and madder as the months that followed went by. Parenthetically, the final arbitrator, the appellate conferee, suggested that I should take 100 percent rather than the 90 percent I claimed! My response was as you would expect, since I am consistent as distinct from these sorts. I said, "Since this is not a mathematical consideration, I will take it up with the regional conferee."

The supportive guy, who by his mere presence was denying her capabilities, had just one thing to say: "I want to see your utility bills and vehicle gas receipts." My office being in the basement, I shouted up to co-taxpayer to fetch those relating to the car, since those for the truck and tractor were in the farm voucher file in my study where they belong and where we were. While we were listening to the pitter-patter of the potentially criminal feet overhead going to her household file, the nonpregnant one of the two examiners said, "Never mind." Can you imagine that? Naturally we were crestfallen. After a few amenities with me probably discussing the pleasant weather, they left with my journals, vouchers, and checking accounts. *They are blind guides, and if one blind man guides another, they will both fall into the ditch.*[3]

They came once more but an accounting of this would just be repetitive.

They reminded me of this story: *Question: If an Indian, a Frenchman and a Polack went skydiving together and none of their chutes opened, who would be the last to reach the ground? Answer: The Polack, because he had to stop to get directions.*[4]

AT NO TIME WAS THERE ANY DISCUSSION OF MY PROFESSIONAL ACCOUNTS.

In August, I received a *52-page audit,* some of it old saw, about a legitimate annuity, which they were still angry about from years back, having been declared wrong by the technical division of the IRS in Washington.

On the first page for 1966, the auditor summarized her disallowances for our local farm as follows:

1) Depreciation	$1,626.83
2) Farm Expenses	3,722.79
3) Farm Loss	1,740.77

This totals $7,090.39, and since the claim was: the money was not used for cattle, then it *must* have been used to stable and feed my child's horse for just one year! If you can figure it any other way, I'm listening.

The audits for the next two of the three years were just as poor. I refused to accept them and obtained an interview with a district conferee. This turned out to be the same conferee whom I had had for the immediately preceding farce (excuse me, audit).

Can you make any sense out of a system which disallows the same auditor on two successive examinations, but does allow the same conferee? What goes on—is he bonded and the lowest echelon not? Has he passed a more suitable FBI test?

Look, I was not objecting. This was the Fed that I had asked for in my letter. We had a good two-hour session, and when I left his office I thought surely since I had changed nothing since the 1965 review in the way I kept my books or operated the farm, as a reasonable person expecting some consistency at this level from someone who had been reasonable quite recently, that the affair would be settled promptly by him. Actually, try to follow this inanity: he reversed *himself* on the annuity that had been approved by him after he consulted the Washington office. He concurred with every one of the hundreds of alterations the auditor had made in my accounts to please her will and also, I suspect, to strike back at me for not wanting her performance, which was pure meddling. The great one declares she had not made one mistake. In his words, he "failed to find any substantial error in the adjustments proposed by the examining officer [what kind of officer—Gestapo?], in respect to your farm operation for the years under review and she is sustained in her findings." What superb gall! He also found that my excellent books were no good and applied penalties for that. I don't recall him ever seeing the books. The only difference between the journal of 1965 and those of the contested years is the dates on the outside covers. He found nothing peculiar about the agent who I mentioned during our session as having handled barbed wire as a pleasure-horse expense for four miles and then apparently got tired of transferring barbed wire from a horse expense, after awhile, leaving some for the cattle. He took no account of the few examples I gave him. *The commandment is, Thou shalt do no theft, and included in the meaning of the same, all wrongful usurpation of another man's goods either by fraud or guile, or by usury, or by violence, or by fear.*[5]

If he had studied the books and compared them page by page with the entries as made on the audit sheets, then this is what he would have seen and this is that in which he concurred. The entries below are from a relatively typical page of the auditor's long digest on which she transcribed her analyses of each of my farm entries to the way she sought them to be. (Refer to page 44.)

Somehow, his "study" as a "reasonable" conferee consumed two months, and in that time he could not find that the auditor enclosed the horses with both barbed-wire and electric fencing, that she disregarded clear division of capital labor and supplies from general expenses. It is plainly evident from this sheet that she did not care whether the expense was depreciable or not because she started with her objective in mind to put the expenses into a nondeductible column, anyway.

The astute conferee, anticipating that I would not stop with him if he rendered an adverse opinion, enclosed forms for an appellate hearing.

Ralph and Sarah Whitely
Exhibit C
Page 4

Description	Amount	Cattle	Horses or Personal	Truck Auto	All Others
8/14 Mr.B fence holes	12.00		12.00		
? Mr. C. Trucking; barn	160.36		32.50		127.86
12/23 D.W. Feeding	15.00				15.00
June Labor. D.W. General	45.00				45.00
Fence	114.75		114.75		
June Labor. D.W. General	37.50				37.50
June Labor. D.W. Fence	97.50		97.50		
Aug. Labor D.W. General	126.00				126.00
Aug. Labor D.W. Fence	66.75		66.75		
Aug. Labor D.C. General	70.63				70.63
Aug. Labor D.C. Fence	36.87		36.87		
Aug. Labor D.C. Bonus	12.50				12.50
5/6 E.J. Plowing	150.00				150.00
9/1 × Hardware. Barb. wire	55.08		55.08		
9/1 × Hardware misc. spls.	9.65				9.65
10/1 × Hardware. Barb. wire	27.80		27.80		
9/10 × lumber Co. lumb	17.68		17.68		
7/30 × Hardw. Barb. wire	20.66		20.66		
6/25 × Hardw. Fencing, perm.	100.30		100.30		
6/25 × Hardw. spls.	.65				.65
6/25 × Hardw. Temp. fence	9.50				9.50
6/25 × Hardw. Tools	3.75				3.75
6/15 rent auger	7.14		7.14		
Feb. Mr. C.C.	20.50		20.50		
to barn repair	6.44		6.44		
May battery, elec. fence	3.95		3.95		
May feed troughs	26.00		26.00		
May new fence	43.75		43.75		
4/20 Mr. C.C. lumber	39.17		39.17		
1/5 Mr. M.G. Elect.	18.95		18.95		
1/7 × Hardw. barb. wire	9.00		9.00		
1/3 Mr. C.C. Gen. labor	62.50		62.50		
1/3 Mr. C.C. Barn labor	76.00		76.00		
1/3 Mr. C.C. Barn material	120.50		120.50		
TOTALS	1,623.83	000	1,015.79	000	608.04

In due time (which means another month) I received notification from a conferee on the appeal level suggesting a meeting in 22 days. The letter is a form one so I will not reproduce it. It does point out that we may present facts, arguments, and legal authority to support our position, and if I want to send them material, that had to arrive five days before the conference.

I knew darn well that I couldn't do in seventeen days what had to be done. So I wrote to him for a delay, taking the opportunity to tell him indirectly what to expect.

5000 15th Street
Pomona, Midamerica
March 4, 1970

Mr. John B. Nice
Appellate Conferee
Appellate Division, IRS
P.O. Box 4444
Midtown, Midamerica

Dear Mr. Nice:

Mrs. Whitely and I thank you for your prompt letter following our decision not to accept the "findings" of auditor and conferee.

It is now March 4th. I am planning a number of affidavits, hopefully some from representatives of the Federal Government. Because of professional pressures, absence of my associate, dying calves and cows on my cow-calf farm, I reluctantly admit that I cannot meet the suggested appointment date with any degree of equanimity remaining to me.

May I suggest a delay of about three weeks—about mid-April?

Appreciatively,
Roger Whitely, M.D.

During the next thirty days, an already wearied taxpayer wrote and assembled the 101-page rebuttal to their 52-page audit. Instead of tit-for-tat, two for one.

Where I obtained the time, I do not know, but find
enough I did, to try to shake the whole region, up to the district director. First I wrote the nonexistent chief of the local
office stating that I wanted affidavits from him about his
personnel as well as affidavits from two of them. He sent
this also to the ethereal but ubiquitous group supervisor via
an internal memo. (I couldn't get him on paper.)

Please read the response:

Address any reply to:

> U.S. Treasury Department
> District Director
> Internal Revenue Service
> Date: Spring, 1970

Roger Whitely, M.D.
5000 15th Street
Pomona, Midamerica

Dear Dr. Whitely:

Agent J. Cicada, Pomona, Midamerica, has sent me
a memo regarding that you wish to request certain affidavits from personnel of the Pomona office. I wish to
inform you that agents are not permitted to sign affidavits in an income tax case except with the express
permission of the District Director's office at Midtown.

It would be appreciated if you would refer any further questions regarding the recent examination of your
income tax returns to the undersigned, or to Mr.
Crackpot at Midtown.

> Sincerely yours,
> *Signature*
> Group Supervisor

Somehow, this response finally provoked my anger, and
I responded the day of receipt; pretty bitter was I. Copies
went to the district director, my lawyer, three accounting
firms handling my affairs over the years, including farm ac-

counts, the local "senior agent," and the regional conferee, as well as the appellate conferee.

I knew from Aristotle that *It is easy to fly into a passion—anybody can do that—but to be angry with the right person to the right extent and at the right time and with the right object and in the right way—that is not easy, and it is not everyone who can do it.*[6]

I also knew that angry men are *Blind and foolish, for reason at such a time takes flight and, in her absence, wrath plunders all the riches of the intellect, while the judgment remains the prisoner of its own pride.*[7] I was hoping that Henry Ward Beecher was right that *A man that does not know how to be angry does not know how to be good.*[8]

I once had a friend, who, speaking about a third friend, said, "John does not know how to be happy unless he is unhappy." It may be true that *Th' next pleasantest feeling in the wurruld to bein' perfectly happy is bein' perfectly cross.*[9] So I took Mark Twain's advice that *When angry, count four; when very angry swear.*[10] I swore without cursing.

5000 15th Street
Pomona, Midamerica
March 18, 1970

Mr. New C. Ants
Group Supervisor
Through Mr. Cicada
Internal Revenue Service
927 Versailles Street
Pomona, Midamerica.

Dear Mr. Ants:

This letter is not to Mr. Cicada. A study of your envelopes and letter heads will indicate the need for this routing.

This is my fourth draft since 8:00 P.M. last night, reception date of your letter.

Please also study your A:F: 1000 Feb. 25, 1970 letter, while rereading your March 16, 1970 letter. The contrasting recommendations about future letters from me are striking. You of course realize that this case has advanced above Mr. Crackpot, conferee. Reference is also made to paragraph (1) IRS publication 5 (Rev.1–69).

Since neither auditor nor conferee *will permit* themselves to see the fruitlessness of declaring that a cattle neck chain is not a cattle neck chain, I believe that your optimum assistance will be to determine whether the scheduled meeting with the appellate conferee will be meaningful. To help you with such decision, I tell you that I do not intend to compromise about whether a cattle neck chain is a cattle neck chain or for personal adornment. I do not intend to concur that one half of a 1/4 million pounds of agricultural lime is for pleasure purposes. I will not deprecate the authoritative counsel of former accountants by concurring that they were incorrect and should have depreciated over 8 years but thirteen (13) dollars of a $113.00 cost basis for a brood cow. I will not concur that a purchase of a mixture of 900 lbs. of crushed corn, 100 lbs. of steer fattener, 4 lbs. of salt and 1 lb. of vitamin A is not for cattle but for horses or personal use. I intend to show inconsistencies in successive audits. I will make every effort to obtain appropriate affidavits from your supervised group of Misters Phil Mein and Crackpot and Mrs. N. Olittle. If their decisions and comments important to me cannot be obtained by a simple expedient of affidavits (as I am required for submission of statements by non-IRS personnel), I will need take an alternate route. Sir, this is simply a statement of my policy.

In part due to this extremely peculiar audit, I have this past week resigned my position as director of a medical department, for I am sickened by the persistent contestation of my compensation.

For you to visualize me better and to aid you in determining the best approach, I tell you I have my own philosophies about my country; it matters little whether I fight for it in the European Theatre or in Vietnam or here. I am in two small businesses, legitimate, and have started a third. I will defend my right to engage in all. I am not intimidated by 52 page audits. Despite N. Olittles, Crackpots, cattle quarantines and weather, I will not let the farm go down the drain as has the directorship. I will resist because the audit is as cruel as it is unconscionable. It also accuses me of stupidity, spending $7,000.00 to feed a child's pet in one year.

I have in preparation a letter to Mr. Nice inquiring whether Xerox copies of more than a score of affidavits will be admissable. I would wish to hold on to the originals unless assured they will be returned immediately after conference(s) if held. If you have the answer to this, please advise and I will not bother him.

Are my spouse and I permitted to submit affidavits?

Please establish for me from undoubtedly readily available statistics the pro rata instances of audited physicians' farm accounts among physicians with farms in this county and other categorizable groups of persons.

Very truly yours
Roger Whitely, M.D.

CC:

   1—Jim Dandy, Director of Internal Revenue, Midtown
     1—Attorney George Crane
     1—Cliffdwellers and Kucher, local office
     1—A.B. Cade, accountant, Honeysuckle, Alabama
     1—Bob Kevan, Doctors' Management
     1—J. Cicada
     1—Blondie N.Olittle
     1—Phil Mein
     1—John B. Nice
     1—Audit file #3

P.S. I take your advice and write directly to Mr. Jim Dandy.

I was provoked because my affidavits from others than the IRS were pouring in in time for me to meet my deadline, but I could not get an affidavit about conversations or statements of experience on any of the IRS agents, again eating up your money and my time.

Using then his statement that the district director can approve such letters sworn under penalty like they make every one of us taxpayers swear on the 1040 form, I sent a letter by special delivery messenger to the director. This outlines what I wanted. He knew that if I got these testimonies I would make the whole organization look as asinine as it is.

5000 15th Street
Pomona, Midamerica
March 19, 1975

Mr. Jim Dandy
District Director of Internal Revenue
100 Post Office Building
Midtown, Midamerica

Dear Mr. Dandy:

This is sent directly to you rather than some subordinate, by registered post or messenger.

I need promptly your express permission to obtain affidavits from some of your personnel as follows:

1) From J. Cicada: an affidavit fully describing the length and breadth of federal income tax experience and the general business experience of auditor Mrs. Blondie N. Olittle with special reference to farm accounts auditing, prior to February, 1969. Also an analysis of why two auditors in the same local office treat differently for tax purposes the trade of one second hand partially depreciated truck for another second hand truck with different end results tax-wise.

2) From Mrs. Blondie N. Olittle: an affidavit regarding statements made by her to my spouse and co-taxpayer, Sarah Whitely, during telephone communication after delivery of audit for the years 1966, 1967, and 1968 to the effect that since she did not know what to do with some of my farm journal entries she arbitrarily divided many of these between horses, personal or not determinable.

3) From I. M. Crackpot: An affidavit that when as

conferee for a 1964–1965 audit he stated that a profit need not be shown on such a farm in five years but that progress must be made. The reason for inattention to my submitted figures to him late in 1969 that the farm in question does show not only progress but anticipated profit in its fourth year. The reason he, as a representative of the IRS, does not know whether were I to add a brood mare as a capital item to my brood cow stock, in 1969, this would or would not be a deductible business expense. The reason that he felt obliged to consult the technical division in Washington in regard to my administrative emolument during 1964 and 1965, answer received from Washington as late as March 18, 1968, but in 1969 despite no change in contractual agreement between taxpayer and same hospital he needs no assistance from Washington, changes in the laws of the land in the intervening period not occurring, and reverses his opinion. The reason that he concurs with auditor N. Olittle that a cow neck chain is not fully a cow neck chain and other items ad infinitum, a few mentioned in accompanying copy letter. The reason that a several-hundred-dollar fence is claimed to be above a $2,000 cost and although approved as a business capital expenditure for 1965 by him is not allowable as an item of business in 1966, 1967, and 1968. The reason that he concurs with aforementioned auditor in the application of penalties for the manner in which I have kept my books based on such inconceivable alterations by her as you will note in attached letter copy. The reason that there is conveniently overlooked over 20,000 uncontested medical business entries for the audited years. The reason why as conferee in audited years 1964 and 1965 he contested no Alabama or Midamerica farm entries.

4) From Phil Mein: an affidavit why he did not know during the 1964–1965 audit that all cows were not born on the same day (and therefore logically have a different depreciable life). The reason and procedures he used in consultation with other IRS personnel in the 1965 audit of my Midamerica farm to establish the business life of my farm building as fifteen years, which

then went uncontested as a business property by himself and others. The reason he would surmise it is now contested by his co-worker in the same local IRS office.

Very truly yours,
Roger Whitely, M.D.

Enclosure:
    Attached letter to:
    New C. Ants, March 18, 1970
cc:
    1—Mr. John B. Nice
    1—Mr. New C. Ants

On March 25 he responded. Read it. Is the group supervisor distorting or is the district director covering up? How can it be that a group supervisor will advise me that affidavits are possible and the superboss of the whole bejizus area can say that "existing procedures do not permit them"? Aren't these persons marching in the same miserable army? Don't they have the same regulations? Is one of them using the French tax system? The director states that I can submit facts, but he conceals from the appellate division facts I want, by majestically refusing to let the facts come to the light of day.

U.S. Treasury Department
District Director
Internal Revenue Service
A City, USA
Spring, 1970

Roger Whitely, M.D.
5000 15th Street
Pomona, Midamerica

Dear Dr. Whitely:

I have carefully reviewed your request for permission to obtain affidavits from certain employees of the

Internal Revenue Service, as identified in your letter of
March 19, 1970. Existing procedures do not permit my
granting your request.

Your case is now under the jurisdiction of the
Chief, Appellate Division, Room 400 Fidelity Building,
Midtown, Midamerica. You may request a hearing before a representative of that Division and submit fac-
tual information, law and argument and/or court decisions which support your position in the recent examination of your 1966, 1967 and 1968 Federal Income Tax
returns.

Any further correspondence should be made directly to that office.

> Sincerely yours,
> *Signature*
> District Director

Maybe your publisher can find out who of the two is telling it the way it is. I would rather enjoy the paradoxical
statements for which the Irish are famous in which two op-
posite concepts bear anyway a logical relationship. *O'Shay
had been having a bitter argument with a friend, and now he
was about to finish him off once and for all. "The sooner I
never see your face again," said O'Shay, "the better it will be
for both of us when we meet!"*[11]
I kept firing letters to the nuisance, Mr. New C. Ants,
the group supervisor. I knew he was out of range, but it
seemed important to me that he begin to judge himself so
that if you went his same way or I did again, he would have
been starched up a bit. I had been using these letters to
place things in them that I wanted the district director to
know about his own organization—what the grass roots were
like—and I wanted the appellate division to learn the policy
I would be following when we finally met. I think this sort of
thing is called a Ciceronion omission. The letter was purely
facetious.

5000 15th Street
Pomona, Midamerica
March 27, 1970

Mr. New C. Ants
Group Supervisor
Internal Revenue Service
Office of the District Director

Dear Mr. Ants:

I have located a letter of February 12, 1969, indicating that your office is in Midtown. You have indicated that I should write to you for advice.

I have a letter received today from the General Agency, U.S.A., Peoria, Southland. This letter is for reference to my audit for the 1966, 1967 and 1968 years. The body of the letter indicates the value of the timber on property that I held in Alabama. You probably know that the auditor disallowed a deduction from sale price of timber since she (Mrs. N. Olittle) claims I had no verification of cost. It turns out that the timber cruise by the Federal Government is greater than the timber cruise made on this property by private people.

This letter is signed by the assistant chief of the Division. He did not place on the letter a signature under penalty of perjury and he did not have his signature notarized.

Please advise me whether I should send this letter back for notarization or whether the federal Internal Revenue Service will accept this other federal letter.

Very truly yours,
Roger Whitely, M.D.

Proclaim the message, press it home on all occasions, convenient or inconvenient, use argument, reproof, and appeal, with all the patience that the work of teaching requires.[12]

After that he bought out. I copy his letter here only that you will see that one irate taxpayer got the IRS to buy a rubber address stamp. Look at the address. He had been concealing himself in the district director's office on his letterhead and it turned out his office was 120 miles south!

Address any reply to:

U.S. Treasury Department

A City, U.S.A.

District Director
Internal Revenue Service
Date: Spring, 1970

Roger Whitely, M.D.
5000 15th Street
Pomona, Midamerica

Dear Dr. Whitely:

Please refer to Mr. Dandy's letter of March 25 in which he states that any further correspondence regarding your case should be made to the office of the Chief, Appellate Division, Midtown, Midamerica. In accordance with these instructions, I am referring your letter of March 17 to Mr. J. B. Nice of that office.

Sincerely yours,
Signature
Group Supervisor

I figured I ought to push on the appellate conferee a little bit; there seemed little harm that could be done by this. I let him know without saying so directly that since this closed-circuit system I was working against was concealing evidence, we—wife and I—were ready to bring it forth with statements signed in such fashion that if incorrect we could be put in jail. We would present what auditors and others had told us by quoting them. Please note that I also asked whether or not the auditor could be brought to the hearing to be questioned by me. I again sent copies to everyone along the long tiresome ambiguous trail. *"Preach not because you have to say something but because you have something to say."*[13]

5000 15th Street
Pomona, Midamerica
April 2, 1970

Mr. John B Nice
Appellate Conferee
Internal Revenue Service
P.O. Box 4444
Midtown, Midamerica   Refer to: L.A. Ap:IN:JBN

Dear Mr. Nice:

I find myself in a quandry.

Your letter states that facts should be in the form of affidavits (or signature under penalty).

(1) Mr. Jim Dandy will not allow me to obtain affidavits from IRS employees.

(2) A Midtown private investigative bureau first accepted an assignment from me at 9 A.M. and then called me back to say that they would not inquire into the business and auditing background of IRS auditor N. Olittle. (FEAR?) The only thing I got from them was "I admire you."

(3) I have asked Mr. New C. Ants whether Mrs. Whitely and I are allowed to sign affidavits on our own behalf since we cannot get the data from IRS personnel. Mr. Ants did not answer this.

Please advise.

Are you in a position to have Mrs. Blondie N. Olittle give testimony at the hearing?

Very truly yours,
Roger Whitely, M.D.

cc:

1—Mrs. Blondie N. Olittle
1—Mr. Jim Dandy

56

1—Mr. New C. Ants
1—Mr. Cicada
1—Mr. George Crane. Lawyer
1—Audit File #3

No answer came, by mail! Did I damage the case? No. Telephone again. We could present statements under penalty of perjury if we wished. He would not allow testimony from the auditor. He inferred (I kept notes of the telecommunication) that the auditor's testimony was unimportant now. I responded that I could never agree with this since the audit would not have been in this disarray if the auditor had been competent.

Well, besides the prologue some pages back, what else did the beleaguered taxpayers prepare for the conferee beyond what he already had from us in direct letters and indirectly in copies of the letters you have seen?

PART III

THE STORY AS WRITTEN TO THE APPELLATE CONFEREE

Few things are of themselves impossible,
And we lack the application to make them a success
Rather than the means.

–*La Rochefoucauld,* Maxims

Chapter IV

STRAIGHT TALK

Sir, the far greater portion of the 52-page audit for the 1966, 1967 and 1968 tax years concerns a farm in Alabama of 117 acres and a farm in Midamerica of 129 acres. I have had another farm in Alabama until 1969 but since this had no cattle on it no auditing "errors" could be found.

The 1945 statute in this country for the years under consideration concern the expenses of business farms which have over a $50,000.00 loss.

Therefore, the case of the auditor and conferee had to be based on a disallowance of expenses by simply baldly stating that much of the expense is for a pleasure motive rather than a profit motive. The auditor and, to my absolute amazement, the conferee are in agreement including a general condemnation of my farm records. They are not in a position to say that the entire expense of the farm is a hobby but attempt to throw legitimate expenses of a cow-calf operation into a pleasure category or personal category or "show horse" category. (See photograph.) You will note that this is done by arbitrarily and unreasonably placing actual cattle expenses into audited columns labeled a) horses and b) variously as follows: "joint expenses"; "all others"; "no heading"; "?"; "undetermined"; "other." (See audit.) Not only is excessive expense placed in her

"horse" column, much of it being for cattle, but extensive insertions which are not indeterminate are placed in the (?) column and the other variety of columns already extensively enumerated above. Then at the end through some magical formula, the derivation of which is not defined anywhere in the audit, and which therefore is purely arbitrary, the sum is split between allowable and not allowable.

It must be realized that a physician has a good amount of general energy and a moderate amount of diverse knowledge. In my own instance, beginning as early as 1961, I wished to determine whether in this single life span one could be productive not only in medicine and teaching but productive in the form of producing a profit in another business. In other words, can one make money in this country, if he be a physician, in other affairs rather than only in medicine? There are some of us who wish challenges. Others, like one of the auditors, suggested to me that I work for the hospital for a salary and that then I would not have the problem of an audit! In the instance of a physician, he is primarily a biologist; medicine is a minor portion of total biology. It is not unreasonable, therefore, that his attention is directed to biological aspects within the business world.

There will be no attempt to belabor you with each separate item in this extraordinarily extensive audit; rather the intent on the part of the taxpayers will be to show the unreasonableness, incorrectness and utterly incomprehensible audaciousness of the decisions made by the aforementioned auditor and conferee as well as their inconsistencies and to supply you with examples.

Please refer to the enclosure I am submitting as an example of how the inexperienced auditor handled just those purchases relating to Grain Marketing Association, Inc. during 1968. Please and I urge you, please, to note that for the entire year the only allowance she permits directly for cattle is the magnificent sum of $10.20.

A CONTRAST IN THE RECOGNITION OF FARM
PURCHASES BY TAXPAYERS
versus
AUDITOR
re: monthly vouchers from Grain Marketing Assn., Inc.

| Items | Taxpayers | | Auditor | | |
	CATTLE	HORSES	CATTLE	HORSES PERSONAL	UNDETERMINED OR?
TOTALS	$1,792.41	$266.12	$10.20	$267.68	$1,781.08

(Editor's note: three pages of items were submitted to the appellate division. These are condensed in the table to show simply the totals in each category. The cattle feed formula consisted of crushed corn, steer chow, vitamins, and salt. All such entries were placed in the undetermined column by the auditor. Also over $1,000 for bulk fertilizer were placed there as well as medicine for the treatment of cattle pinkeye, cattle fly dusts, cattle identification chains with numbered tags, etc. It was not possible to determine from the auditor's notes what item costing $10.20 she did allow for cattle during the entire year.)

Over the years since submitting this to the conferee I have often wondered why the auditor laboriously transcribed my entries to her audit sheets. She might have just as well picked some dollar sum from the air and then placed the thousands of dollars into the indeterminate and personal columns.

Mr. Conferee, in the same year, the auditor permits no hay purchases as identifiable for cattle. I am at this point of this draft in my 119th hour since first hearing from you, so forgive me if my fatigue overcomes my courtesy when I state that either the SPCA should put me in jail now or I should be in jail via the IRS for depreciating dead cows! NO HAY! NO GRAIN! as clearly recognizable expenses for cattle. Is not the maturity of the regional conferee supposed to stop such nonsense?

Does anyone dare say, anyone, that these assertions by them are "reasonable"? Is it reasonable for me to waste my time with counterclaims against non-claims?

Apparently, the auditor either overlooked or failed to inquire on the basis of my returns that the figure on the return, for instance of feed, is less than the annual feed bill which is in my journal and which I will bring for you. It is my belief that she did not even bother to add these up for comparative purposes to see if the taxpayer was cognizant that from one to one and a half horses were surely not deductible from taxes. *I know* that a pleasure horse is not a tax deductible item. My books will show this. She concluded without requesting of Mrs. Whitely or myself how we approached this non-deductible expense. She simply decided that we were willfully deceptive.

I wrote the auditor originally to prepare a list of any mathematical or accounting errors. It was my intent to pay such immediately. I also requested of her to prepare a list of other inquiries (of a debative or argumentative category). I preferred that these latter go to conference. The reason for this letter to her will be evident to you. It is substantiated in this brief.

I do not concur, and never will, that the auditor's figures, using as an example the year 1966, are correct. You will note that her figures indicate that the pleasure horse cost us $7,090.39, plus the work of my wife, plus the work of my daughter, plus very little work from me, plus the cost of items purchased that were not placed in the journal (not expensed). Since a horse can be stabled in this county for $600.00 a year and since this stabling includes labor and feed and other incidental expenses, the auditor is off by far greater than 1200%.

Do we have an expert to substantiate this? Yes.

> BARREN HILL STABLE
> R.R. 10
> Pomona, Midamerica
> March 18, 1970

Mr. John B. Nice
Appellate Conferee
Internal Revenue Service

Dear Mr. Nice:

I am the professional trainer and co-manager of the Barren Hill Stable in Pomona, Midamerica. I have been the advisor for Dr. and Mrs. Roger Whitely on the purchases of all their horses.

The first one was purchased in August, 1963 for $650.00 for their then 11-year-old daughter. I taught her to ride. She subsequently showed the horse in the local fair horse shows as do many County 4-H children. This horse cannot be classified as a "show horse" in the sense that a professional horseman would define the term. He is now 11 years old and has been lame for years.

The second horse they purchased was one for the doctor in April, 1965 just before the purchase of his farm. The purchase price was $240.00 including a saddle and bridle. It is of nondescript type but very suitable for his purposes—a farm animal to ride the fence lines, count cattle and to search for newborn calves. Both of these animals were stabled at the above stable from the time of their purchase until December 24, 1965. Our charge was $50.00 per month for the child's gelding for which we provided a stall and $30.00 a month for the doctor's mare which was at pasture.

Under penalty of perjury I declare I have examined this statement and to the best of my knowledge, believe it is true and accurate.

Very truly yours
A.S. Expert

I assure you that if there be any errors on our part not counterbalanced by other not expensed items, that this error will not run that high. Those errors of ours that may be present, although they should not have occurred will still not be unreasonable. The auditor's claims are unreasonable. Had she no concept of the horse-cattle ratio?

The auditor claims that "Farm experts in this area have stated that there is no possibility for a profit with an operation of this size." The conferee concurs with this quotation as follows: "A profit motive has not been substantiated and personal motives are dominant." I am unable to resist, sir, placing in on this last draft for you to note this remarkable clairvoyance. I agree that if I am so incapable that I permit myself to waste $7,090.39 to feed and house a horse that I will not make money proportionally on approximately 35 brood cows; assuming the costs to feed a cow and maintain such unit is *one-fourth* that of a horse, I will go broke in less than a year paying $61,000.00 to sustain the cows and calves. This proportionate argument is reasonable. More to the point, I used all the figures that she allowed as allowable expense for the cattle and I then inserted her figures into farm Form F returns to test her credibility. The outcome is as follows:

DERIVATION OF MIDAMERICA FARM LOSSES AND GAINS
EMPLOYING FIGURES OF AUDITOR
1966 Returns

Income	Expenses per Return	Disallowed by Auditor
$3,030.22	7,582.26 Regular	3,722.79 Expenses
	2,690.39 Depreciation	1,626.83 Depreciation
		1,740.77 Losses
	$10,272.65	7,090.39

$10,272.65 minus 7,090.39 = $3,182.26 Allowed
3,030.22 minus 3,182.26 = $152.04 *Loss* in first
full year of operation, after converting grain farm to cow-calf farm.

1967 Returns

Income	Expenses per Return	Disallowed by Auditor
$3,818.01	6,516.88 Regular	3,776.96 Expenses
	2,639.97 Depreciation	1,606.09 Depreciation
	9,156.85	5,383.05

$9,156.85 minus $5,383.05 = $3,773.80 Allowed
$3,818.01 minus 3,773.80 =   44.21 Gain in second
year.

1968 Returns

Income	Expenses per Return	Disallowed by Auditor
$3,899.94	6,555.87 Regular	$3,274.78 Expenses
	2,977.01 Depreciation	1,910.32 Depreciation
		446.84 Loss
	$9,532.88	5,631.94

$9,532.88 minus $5,631.94 = $3,900.94 Allowed
$3,899.94 minus $3,900.94 = $ 1.00 *Loss* in third
year
(The purchase of two bales of hay less would produce a
profit!)

Conclusions: Her own figures refute her own categoric statements.

The auditor cannot substantiate her own experts.

Well, Mr. Interlocutor, do you see any semblance of reason here? *Peace rules the day when reason rules the mind.*[1] *To a reasonable creature, that alone is insupportable which is unreasonable; but everything reasonable may be supported.*[2] *'Tis in vain to speak of reason where 'twill not be heard.*[3] *Reason cannot save us, nothing can; but reason can mitigate the cruelty of living.*[4]

It is of particular interest to me that I could be so deceiving on the Midamerica farm for these three audited years but that I had no farm discrepancies in any previously audited years; in other words, there was nothing wrong on December 31, 1965, but on January 1, 1966, there are scores of pages of features considered serious discrepancies; that there are no cheatings in our hundreds of thousands of dollars of gross professional income, in the thousands of dollars returned or not returned of overpayments by patients in the form of credits; that there is nothing wrong with scores upon scores of stock transactions or oil drilling ventures.

U.S. TREASURY DEPARTMENT
Internal Revenue Service
District Director
A City, USA
Spring, 1968

Dr. and Mrs. Roger Whitely
5000 15th Street
Pomona, Midamerica

Dear Dr. and Mrs. Whitely:

As a result of technical advice received from our National Office, we are conceding the $6,000.00 adjustment proposed on your 1964 and 1965 Federal income tax returns. Your returns have therefore been adjusted as shown in the attached Conference Audit Statement, which supplements the revenue agent's report

Very truly yours,
Signature
Chief, Technical Branch

Suddenly, like a leopard changing spots, I attempt to take advantage of my country only in regard to farms. The dove becomes a limited hawk with only farm prey in mind; the farm hawk begins to do some skimming. The hawk, though, being feeble-minded, puts stalls on the road side of the barn for auditors to see but then conceals expenses of about $18,000.00 by peculiar bookkeeping.

Here is how she does this! A child can uncover the ruse. In 1965 a total of $2,095.52 was spent (and depreciated) for miles upon miles of barbed wire fencing and some short section of wood fencing. This tax year was audited and there was *no* discrepancy in this item. This untrained auditor then takes this same figure, states it was purely for wooden fencing (what the dickens has been keeping the cows locked into the 129 acres?) around a small holding pasture, and disallows it in its entirety because it is "used exclusively for pleasure." The same with the barn!

It is unknown to me the reason that a several hundred dollar fence is claimed by her to cost $2,095.52 (affidavit refused). And what about this pasture anyway? Am I not allowed to have a small pasture? Am I not allowed to have a beautiful small pasture? The paddock within it is incidental, not its purpose. The horses are incidental to the 129 acre farm business, not the *present* purpose of the farm. The wood enclosing the paddock does not interfere with the basic purposes of the pasture. Do you notice who selected this wood which was cut on this farm for this fencing?

Let's hear about the wood enclosed pasture from a reverend who is a part-time carpenter. Later, you will learn what the occupation is of the gentleman who

69

selected the trees on the farm for the wood fencing for
this "contested" pasture.

*That a man should eat and drink and enjoy himself, in
return for all his labors, is a gift of God.*[5]

Rural Route 2
Pomona, Midamerica
March 16, 1970

Mr. John B. Nice
Appellate Division
Internal Revenue Service

Sir:

I am the contractor who performed the major portion of the carpentry work on the barn and a small pasture enclosed by a wooden fence on the French Township farm of Dr. Roger Whitely.

The barn design is unusual. It is the doctor's own
design. It is the best one I have ever built or repaired.
It has flexibility built into it, so as the years go by, it
can be used for more than one purpose. The barn has a
square base footage of 2880 feet. It has been expanded
to 3600 square feet with a shed. The shed was not
added until a full two years after the barn was built but
it had been planned for from the beginning. So it puz-
zles me that only the shed can be depreciated. The barn
has cow feed bunkers running 120 feet. It stores about
50 tons of hay. It also stores his equipment and tools.
The square footage for the two horses is 240 feet. So I
cannot understand why it would be declared a horse
barn.

Costs were reduced by Dr. Whitely and his sons
doing some work themselves or helping me. Some of the
feed troughs were constructed of his poplar lumber
which was also used for the contested board fence.

Many fall evenings in 1965, while I was working on
the barn, he would ask me to help him roll out 1/4 mile

of barbed wire. He would staple this up himself and return at dark. We would then turn on the lights and work together on the barn. He had to work this way at nights and weekends to get the farm fenced in in time for delivery of his first thirty brood cows.

I recommended Billy Jim Mosby to Dr. Whitely to cut five poplar trees to proper length for the fence, which trees had been selected by the Soil Conservation officer of our district. This cutting cost Dr. Whitely $30.00. I also arranged for the Poplar Lumber Company to pick up the logs, saw them and return the lumber. This cost $250.15. This figures out less than six (6) cents per board foot. Since four 1" × 6" boards were used to gain suitable height, this makes the fence cost less than twelve (12) cents per foot. *Low* hog wire costs approximately nine (9) cents a foot. He would have needed a couple strands of barbed wire above it. We also would have needed about twenty more corner and pull posts, which would cost approximately $75.00 plus the barbed wire. So I feel that the wooden fence did not cost as much as a wire fence. Dr. Whitely said the auditor assigned a cost of $2,095.52 to the fence. Dr. Whitely put in most of the posts himself. One helper and I nailed the boards up in a few days. I feel that there was an error made in her costs.

For the same money or less, the doctor got a good solid fence, which is also attractive, instead of a wire fence which would not have been contested. Dr. Whitely said that the audit showed that the wooden fence was disallowed. I cannot understand why, when in 1965 he said it was allowed by the auditor of that year.

Originally, the small south pasture was divided in two parts, with a straight north-south fence to help separate the cows if needed. When we finally got the pens and squeeze corridor built, we took down the dividing fence and instead of throwing all of this good lumber away, we used the same posts and boards for a paddock for his thirteen-year-old daughter's use. The cost was very small for extra material and labor and does not in any way interfere with the farm operation.

In this boarded area, I have watched Dr. Whitely wean his calves and the herd graze down as needed.

I have seen both Dr. Whitely and his wife work hard to build the farm to where it is now.

Under penalty of perjury I declare I have examined this statement and to the best of my knowledge believe it is true and accurate.

Reverend A. L. Sound

The mightiest of rivers lose their force when split up into several streams.[6] *Divide the fire, and you will sooner put it out.*[7]

It is known to me that the auditor, Mrs. Blondie N. Olittle, made statements to my spouse and co-taxpayer, Mrs. Sarah Whitely, during a telephone communication after delivery of the audit for the three years to the effect that since *she did not know what to do* with some of my farm journal entries she divided many of them between horses, personal or not determined. The exact statement was requested by an affidavit from her but this was refused by District Director Jim Dandy.

Well, our Lord of the domain would not let us get statements from Mrs. N. Olittle so let's see what co-taxpayer sent to the appellate division to help him in his judgment. She is going to place herself in a position where she can be fined for perjury. My wife is telling of the vagueness and incompetence of the auditor.

5000 15th Street
Pomona, Midamerica
April 10, 1970

Mr. John B. Nice:
Appellate Conferee
Internal Revenue Service

Dear Mr. Nice:

As cotaxpayer, I wish to advise you that the only

information requested of me by the auditor was proof that I had paid the social security taxes for my part-time maid. While Mrs. Olittle and her preceptor were here at our home, he requested our gasoline and telephone receipts from Dr. Whitely. When *I* produced them he did not examine them.

After reviewing the audit and examining the many items the auditor had assigned to personal use or to horses, I telephoned her. Upon questioning her as to her knowledge of feed requirements for one horse, she was vague. I then asked her if she was aware that horses are not usually kept in barbed wire enclosures. This she said she knew as she was raised on a farm. Then we do not understand why she has not in any part allowed the external fencing around the 129 acres and only in part allowed the miles of cross fencing. She then said that there were many items that she did not know what to do with and so placed them in her other columns. She further added that since my husband was very busy, she did not want to bother him. If she had asked me, I would have been glad to work with her on this and would have produced receipts and publications which would show the amounts of feed recommended to feed one 1,200 pound horse. I would have gone over page after page of other items in the audit. I work on the farm too.

As my daughter and I take complete care of and feed the horses as well as some care of the cows and calves, I am well aware of the feed requirements and costs.

Your attention is focused to our reference 12 in the supportive attachments. The grain purchased for horses in 1968 cost $266.12. In that year there were present and fed by us one farm horse, one pet horse, both for a period of 12 months. My brood mare was fed for 5 1/2 months. $266.00 divided by 2.5 equals $106.00 per year grain per horse (but includes as well salt, vitamins, etc.). May I add here that for eight months of any year, Dr. Whitely does not have his cow-calf food mixture available. We feed the bull the horse formula by the pailful and when my husband is alone or with us getting the cattle to the pens for spraying or other attention, he uses this grain also by the multiple pailfuls.

Of the quantity of straw used, it is not expensed; and indeed of this unexpensed straw, a great deal is used for cattle.

Out of personal accounts we also pay all farrier bills, bills for floating teeth and veterinary bills, with possibly one four dollar exception in the three years. You will find the signed statement about the veterinary bills in the attachments. These items, unexpensed, are also for the farm horse as well as the pet.

Under penalty of perjury I declare that I have examined this statement and to the best of my knowledge I believe it is true and accurate.

Very truly yours
Sarah Whitely.

It is known to me that certified public accounting procedures in regard to the depreciation of cattle were accepted by auditors for previous years and now all of a sudden the rules of the game change even among the auditors in the same IRS office (affidavit refused).

It is known to me that a previous auditor for the tax years 1964 and 1965 decided that the depreciation life of the barn of fifteen years is correct and that this was decided in consultation with others of the local office and that they approved the barn as a cow barn in the audited tax year of 1965 (affidavit refused). I and others do not agree even that it is a small barn. It is known to me that the present auditor and conferee claim that no portion of the barn is deductible. It is unknown to me the reason why Mr. Mein would surmise it is now contested by his coworker in the same revenue service office (affidavit refused). It is unknown to me why the same auditor did not know during the periods of his audit that all cows are not born on the same day and, therefore logically, have a different depreciable life at the time of purchase. This affidavit from Mr. Phil Mein was requested by me and refused by Mr. Jim Dandy.

It is known to me that when I needed aid in the preparation of my 1968 return, I asked advice in the local IRS office concerning the trade-in of one second-hand truck for another, did what I was advised, and then the auditor for 1968 changed this completely about from a loss to a gain! The testimonies to this effect are refused by Mr. Jim Dandy.

It is known to me and by persons in the IRS that I requested an experienced auditor because of previous experiences with them in which I had to teach not only the useful life of cows but also in the 1963 tax year that pulpwood, standing, and held for more than six months was not regular income when sold but should be treated as capital gains.

It is known to me that I asked for such experienced auditor after a telephone conversation initiated by Mrs. N. Olittle at the very beginning of this inspection at which time she indicated to me that I had sold an Alabama farm in 1967! I had not. It is known to me that as a consequence of these previous experiences and this telephone discussion, I then asked for an auditor with at least 5 years' experience so that this new accounting would not take seventeen months as did the immediately previous one.

It is known to me that a written testimony from Mr. J. Cicada fully describing the length and breadth of federal tax experience and the general business background of N. Olittle with special reference to farm accounting prior to February, 1969, is refused by Mr. Jim Dandy. It is known to both you and me that a private investigator has refused to get this simple data.

It is unknown to me the reason for the inattention of conferee I. M. Crackpot to my submitted figures to him late in 1969 (affidavit refused) at the time of the present conference with him that the farm in question did not only show progress but an anticipated profit in its fourth year. The content of this thesis indicates that he is the one who told me I do not have to make a profit even by the fifth year.

It is unknown to me why he as a representative of the IRS does not *now* know whether were I to add a brood mare as a capital item to my brood cow stock, in 1970, this would or would not be an acceptable business expense.

I suspect it is easier not to know and simply not allow it by edict at my next and anticipated audit. (I am a doctor.)

I had shown Mr. Crackpot a cancelled check, which I will have with me if you care to see it, for a stud fee but which we did not enter in our journal for 1969 since the mare did not settle. It is known to me that I was looking for some free and accurate and knowledgeable advice, directly from a learned member of the IRS (affidavit refused).

It must be remembered that Mr. Crackpot was recalled by me as a gentleman and an understanding reasonable conferee from the 1964–1965 audit. It is known to me that at the time of that inspection he in effect said, let us get on at the first meeting with the matter of the contested annuity, the remaining piddling (a word more or less of this character) contested farm points can be settled even by telephone. It interests me no end that the items other than the annuity for those two tax years were so minor that they could be settled by telephone but that the piddling (my word now) forty odd pages in regard to the Midamerica farm now being contested are not now piddling to him. How can this be?

It is unknown to me, for instance, the reason that Mr. Crackpot agrees with his junior that a cow neck-chain is not fully a cow neck-chain and why other items are not deductible for approximately 80% of the audit, a few mentioned as examples herewith.

It is unknown to me the reason that the conferee concurs with the auditor in the application of penalties for the manner in which I have kept my books based on such inconceivable alterations by her, as you will note, in her fantasy.

It is unknown to me the reason that the auditor and the conferee conveniently overlooked contesting 22,909 medical financial record entries for the same three years.

I want you to hear from my business managers next. They also are willing to go to jail if and when it can be proved they are lying.

300 First Street
Pomona, Midamerica
March 23, 1970

Mr. John B. Nice
Appellate Conferee
Internal Revenue Service

Dear Mr. Nice:

I am the present business office manager for Dr. Whitely, of this city, and am in charge of billing patients, third parties and in entering collections. I am also supervisor of two clerks who assist me in my duties.

At the request of Dr. Whitely, I have just completed a survey of each page of his day books. These go back to July 1, 1966, which is the same day Medicare went into effect.

On these pages there are entries of the dollars business done, the daily breakdown of the character of professional services rendered into the various categories. There is on the appropriate page for each day, the entries for checks received or cash received, from whom and to what amounts.

He asked me just to add up the numbers of journal entries relating to cash received or checks received, none others.

These are summarized for you:

For 1966	2,664	of such bookkeeping entries
1967	10,012	of such bookkeeping entries
1968	10,233	of such bookkeeping entries

Grand total   22,909

Although I have done this with care and with the aid of an adding machine there may be a plus or minus variation of 3%.

On March 20th, 1970 I questioned my two assistants to learn of them, both having been here during 1969, whether any representative of the Internal Rev-

77

enue Service at any time during 1969 requested of them an opportunity to examine the day sheets of 1966, 1967 and 1968. Neither of them had such a request from anyone representing any governmental branch.

Under penalty of perjury, I declare the statements above are true and accurate to the best of my knowledge.

Very truly yours,
Mrs. June Sike

300 Rosewood Court
Augusta, Alabama
March 24, 1970

Mr. John B. Nice
Appellate Conferee
Internal Revenue Service.

Dear Mr. Nice:

From February 15 through October 31, 1969 I was engaged as business manager for a group of physicians in Pomona, Midamerica. My primary responsibility was to oversee the billings of professional fees. All bills were prepared in the name of Roger Whitely, M.D. and checks from patients and insurance companies were deposited to his account. I was assisted by two women employees who prepared the billing statements. Our business office was located in space rented from the hospital by the physicians.

It was coincidental that during my tenure my father was informed that an audit of his 1966, 1967 and 1968 tax returns would be undertaken by the IRS. Considering this, it is remarkable that the IRS auditor, one Mrs Blondie N. Olittle, never approached me for any of our day pages nor any of our patients' statements either receivable or collected for the years under review. Additionally, I was never asked to produce these records, which I might add are voluminous, for the two audits held at my father's house that I was aware of. It is a matter of fact that neither of my assistants ever advised me that Mrs. N. Olittle requested this information. Indeed, I have never met the lady.

I was instructed by my father at the time of my employment never to disregard my responsibility to keep any and all material pertaining to his professional financial affairs, specifically to ensure that all would be available in the event of an IRS audit. For the record, I wish to state that it would have been a very simple matter to alter our journals so that tens of thousands of dollars of professional income could have been concealed. This, however, is unthinkable considering the ethics and impeccable honesty with which my father has always conducted his affairs. Considering my knowledge of the auditor's claim of improper entry on the farm accounts, it is puzzling that Mrs. N. Olittle did not request to review the professional accounts in the same light.

Under penalty of perjury I declare that I have prepared and examined this statement and to the best of my knowledge I believe it is true and accurate.

Yours very truly,
Randolph J. Whitely

This audit was as complete as that of a car inspection of just the right hand windshield wiper and the horn.

It is unknown to me the reason why, as conferee, Mr. Crackpot for the 1964 and 1965 years contested neither any of the Alabama farm entries which are now being contested nor the 1965 Midamerica farm entries much of which are now being contested, the capital items being the same. Certainly these are inconsistencies.

It is unknown to me why both examiners have refused to consider available evidence at the time they were reviewing my books that a profit was being made in 1969. It is known to me, and now to you, that the net earnings (capital gains, $429.00, plus regular income, $6,625.00, minus the expenses, $3,169.00 minus depreciation $2,988.00) equals $897 and more important that the cash flow equals $3,885.00. It is also known to me that in 1969 in regard to all my farms I am paying taxes on $13,249.00, not a puny sum.

Gains and Losses From Sales or Exchanges of Property

Attach this schedule to your income tax return, Form 1040

1969

Name as shown on page 1 of Form 1040: *Roger + Sarah Whitely*

Social Security Number: *000 00 0000*

Part I—CAPITAL ASSETS—Short-term capital gains and losses—assets held not more than 6 months

a. Kind of property. Indicate security, real estate, or other (Specify)	b. Description (Examples: 100 sh. of "Z" Co., 2 story brick, etc.)	c. How acquired. Enter letter symbol (See instr.)	d. Date acquired (mo., day, yr.)	e. Date sold (mo., day, yr.)	f. Gross sales price	g. Depreciation allowed (or allowable) since acquisition	h. Cost or other basis, cost of subsequent improvements (if not purchased, attach explanation) and expense of sale	i. Gain or loss (f plus g less h)
1								
	See Attached Schedule							(1620)

2 Enter your share of net short-term gain (or loss) from partnerships and fiduciaries . . . .

3 Enter unused short-term capital loss carryover from preceding taxable years (attach statement) . . . .

4 Net short-term gain (or loss) from lines 1, 2, and 3 . . . . • **(1620)**

Long-term capital gains and losses—assets held more than 6 months (12 months or more for certain livestock)

5 Enter gain from Part II, line 3 . . . . **12,352**

a	b	c	d. Date acquired	e. Date sold	f. Gross sales price	g. Depreciation	h. Cost or other basis	i. Gain or loss
Timber			1965	1969	1575		1,111	464
See Attached schedule								(11,312)
Livestock	2 cows		1965	1969	332	209	257	284
Died	2 cows		1967	1969	—	81	400	(319)

Total long-term gross sales price . . [ ]

6a Enter your share of net long-term gain (or loss) from partnerships and fiduciaries . . . .

6b Enter your share of net long-term gain from small business corporations (Subchapter S) . . . .

7 Enter unused long-term capital loss carryover from preceding taxable years (attach statement) . . . . . .

8 Capital gain dividends (see Form 1040 Instructions, page 5) . . . .

9 Net long-term gain (or loss) from lines 5, 6a, 6b, 7, and 8 . . . . **1,469**

10 Combine the amounts shown on lines 4 and 9, and enter the net gain (or loss) here . . . . **(151)**

11 If line 10 shows a GAIN—Enter 50% of line 9 or 50% of line 10, whichever is smaller. (Enter zero if there is a loss or no entry on line 9.) (See reverse side for computation of alternative tax.) . . . .

12 Subtract line 11 from line 10. Enter here and in Part IV, line 1, on reverse side . . . .

13 If line 10 shows a LOSS—Enter here and in Part IV, line 1, the smallest of the following: (a) the amount on line 10; (b) the amount on Form 1040, page 1, line 11b, computed without regard to capital gains or losses; or (c) $1,000 . . . • **(151)**

Part II—GAIN FROM DISPOSITION OF DEPRECIABLE PROPERTY UNDER SECTIONS 1245 AND 1250—assets held more than 6 months (see instructions for definitions)

Where double headings appear, use the first heading for section 1245 and the second heading for section 1250.

a. Kind of property and how acquired (if necessary, attach statement of descriptive details not shown below—write 1245 or 1250 to indicate type of asset)	b. Date acquired (mo., day, yr.)	c. Date sold (mo., day, yr.)	d. Gross sales price	e. Cost or other basis, cost of subsequent improvements (if not purchased, attach explanation) and expense of sale
1 FARM - Lincolnton Co, Alabama	1961	1969	25,300	12,107
FARM - Columbia Co, Alabama	1961	1967	10,200	6,560

f. Depreciation allowed (or allowable) since acquisition		g. Adjusted basis (e less sum of f-1 and f-2)	h. Total gain (d less g)	i. Ordinary gain (lesser of f-2 or h) OR (see instructions)	j. Other gain (h less i)
f-1. Prior to January 1, 1962 OR Prior to January 1, 1964	f-2. After December 31, 1961 OR After December 31, 1963				
	503	11,544	7,756	44	7,712
	—	6,560	3,640		3,640

2 Total ordinary gain. Enter here and in Part IV, line 2, on reverse side . . . . • **44**

3 Total other gain. Enter here and in Part I, line 5; however, if the gains do not exceed the losses when this amount is combined with other gains and losses from section 1231 property enter the total of column j in Part III, line 1 . . **12,352**

SCHEDULE F (Form 1040)

**U.S. Treasury Department
Internal Revenue Service**

Schedule of Farm Income and Expenses

(Compute social security self-employment tax on Schedule F–1 (Form 1040))

Attach this schedule to your income tax return, Form 1040

1969

Name as shown on page 1 of Form 1040: *Roger and Sara Whitely*

Social security number: *000 | 000 | 0000*

Business name and address: *Same as above*

If you filed Form 943, enter employer identification number here

Location of farm(s) and number of acres in each farm: *129 Acres, French Township, Baker County, Midamerica*

FARM INCOME FOR TAXABLE YEAR—CASH RECEIPTS AND DISBURSEMENTS METHOD

PART I.—Report in the applicable column below receipts from sale of livestock held primarily for sale. (Do not include other sales of livestock held for draft, breeding, or dairy purposes; report such sales on Schedule D (Form 1040))

| SALES OF MARKET LIVESTOCK AND PRODUCE RAISED AND HELD PRIMARILY FOR SALE | | | | | | OTHER FARM INCOME | |
Kind	Quantity	1. Amount	Kind	Quantity	2. Amount	Items	3. Amount
Cattle		$ 4968.	Grain		$	Mdse. rec'd for produce	$
			Hay			Machine work	
Sheep			Cotton			Patronage dividends	51 00
Swine			Tobacco			Per-unit retains	
Poultry			Vegetables			Agricultural program payments:	
Bees			Fruits and nuts			(1) In cash	1344 00
Dairy products			Syrup and sugar			(2) In materials and services	
Eggs			Wood and lumber			(3) Commodity Credit loans forfeited (or under election)	
Meat products			Other forest products			Gasoline tax credit	
Poultry, dressed						Other (specify):	
Wool			Other (specify):			*Miscellaneous*	262 00
Honey							
Totals		$ 4968 00			$ 000		$ 1657 00

Total of columns 1, 2, and 3. Enter here and in Part IV, line 1 below . . . . $ 6625 00

PART II.—SALES OF PURCHASED LIVESTOCK AND OTHER ITEMS PURCHASED FOR RESALE

a. Description	b. Date acquired	c. Amount received	d. Cost or other basis	e. Profit (or loss)
Livestock:		$	$	$
Other items:				
Totals (enter amount from column e, in Part IV, line 2 below)		$	$	$

PART III.—FARM EXPENSES FOR TAXABLE YEAR (see separate instructions)

(Do not include personal or living expenses or expenses not attributable to production of farm income, such as taxes, insurance, repairs, etc., on your dwelling)

Items	1. Amount	Items	2. Amount	Items	3. Amount
Labor hired	$ 330	Veterinary, medicine	$ 44	Retirement plans, etc. (Other than your share—See instructions)	$
Repairs, maintenance	52	Gasoline, fuel, oil	325	Other (specify):	
Interest		Storage, warehousing		*Miscellaneous*	291
Feed purchased	992	Taxes	292	*License*	20
Seed, plants purchased		Insurance	157	*F I C A Taxes*	268
Fertilizers, lime		Utilities	87		
Machine hire		Rent of farm, pasture			
Supplies purchased	288	Freight, trucking	21		
Breeding fees		Conservation expenses			

Total of columns 1, 2, and 3. Enter here and in Part IV, line 4 below (cash method), or page 2, Part VII, line 6 (accrual method) . . . . $ 3169

PART IV.—SUMMARY OF INCOME AND DEDUCTIONS—CASH RECEIPTS AND DISBURSEMENTS METHOD

1 Sale of livestock and produce raised and other farm income	$ 6625 —	4 Farm expenses (from Part III)	$ 3169 —
2 Profit (or loss) on sale of purchased livestock and other purchased items		5 Depreciation (from Part V)	2988 —
		6 Other farm deductions (specify):	
3 Gross profits*	$ 6625 —	7 Total deductions	$ 6157 —

8 Net farm profit (or loss) (subtract line 7 from line 3). Enter here and on Form 1040, page 2, Part II, line 6. Figure your self-employment income and tax on Schedule F–1 . . . . $ 468 —

*Use this amount for optional method of computing net earnings from self-employment. (See line 3, Schedule F–1 (Form 1040).) c59—16—80205–1

Here are the schedules F for farm and D for Sales or Exchanges of Property. By the way, we just signed these last week when we submitted the 1040 for 1969. Therefore you have spouse and me under perjury statements, since I am introducing these in support of the farm producing income.

When I make an investment of the type I have on this farm, as I have on others,* I will secure it as best I can with my work, including hard physical labor, beautification, adaptability, expert advice, thrift, timber cruises, land evaluations and product need.

Let me urge you not only to read the following 10 testimonies which support these eight contentions by me, but please note who signed them and note the occupations of these people. Be advised that these are either signatures with a perjury statement or a notarized signature. An exception is a letter from the United States of America. One of its officers signed it. Some of these people are employed by the federal government—county agent, soil conservationist. Others are graduate engineers, one a bank vice-president. It does not really matter. What does matter is that not one of them is afraid of "censure" by the IRS!.

UNITED STATES OF AMERICA
GENERAL AGENCY
Peoria, Southland
March 23, 1970

Roger Whitely, M.D.
5000 15th Street
Pomona, Midamerica

Dear Dr. Whitely:

Reference is made to your letter of March 4, 1970, requesting appraisal information in connection with

---

*I claimed a cost basis for depletion allowance of timber sold from the Alabama farm as $1800.00. I was conservative but the auditor said that even this was unsubstantiated. A *superior* Federal Agency states the cost basis as $6,000!!

Tract ZN-8 at the Majestic Reservoir, Alabama, which you purchased in 1961.

The estimated value of this tract at the time of your purchase was $12,000 (i.e. land—$6,000; timber—$6,000).

We trust this information will suffice.

Sincerely,
Edward Fowler

Frankville, Midamerica
March 17, 1970

Mr. John B. Nice
Appellate Conferee
Internal Revenue Service

Dear Mr. Nice:

I am a full time farmer in Baker County, French Township. In 1965 I seeded Dr. Whitely's first pasture. I plowed the ground, disced, and sowed a seed mixture predominately of fescue with wheat as a cover crop. The County agent and I thought this would make him a pasture that would be early in the spring and also make a late fall pasture for his cow herd. On occasions I have given Dr. Whitely advice on his cow-calf operation.

I have bought feeder calves from the doctor at different times. Feeder calves are in short supply in this area, and it is helpful that he raises them.

I have also sold him hay for his cows. He usually buys 400–500 bales at a time which I deliver and put in the mow of his barn. Mrs. Whitely has also bought hay for the horses. She comes to my farm and picks up 10–20 bales at a time. Dr. Whitely pays for the hay that I deliver and his wife pays for the hay she picks up.

Dr. Whitely has done a lot of manual labor on this farm. He has built fence, feeds the cattle and cleans the barn of manure. I am sure he would not do all of this if he did not expect to make a profit out of his cow and calf operation.

Under the penalty of perjury, I declare that I have examined this statement and to the best of my knowledge, I believe it is true and accurate.

Very truly yours,
George Fair.

3000 Big Oak Drive
Biloxi, Ohio
March 17, 1970

Mr. John B. Nice
Appellate Conferee
Internal Revenue Service

Dear Sir:

I have worked periodically for my father on his farm in the State of Alabama since 1961 and on the farm in Baker County, Midamerica since 1965. Since two of my summer vacations from college have been spent on the latter farm, I am quite familiar with the planning, the construction, the capital and operating expenditures, the actual operation, and the aims of my father in establishing this cow-calf and timber farm. More recently, I have become familiar with the 1966–1968 audit and accounts of his local farm.

Since my graduation from Midamerica Tech in September 1967, I have been employed by the Department of Health, Education and Welfare as a civil engineer. During this thirty month period, I have become familiar with the operations of the Federal Government, including the failures to relate to actual problems as well as the excellent work done by the many capable persons within the various departments. I have resisted vigorously the occasional poor planning, wasteful expenditures, and poor quality output done by persons not yet knowledgeable in the area of assignment. My affidavit presented here is not only an accounting of my work on this Midamerica farm, but also a protest of this audit as what I have referred to as poor quality output.

The Midamerica farm has been characterized by

the desire to create at minimal capital expenditure a profitable and easily maintained and operated cow-calf program while retaining within this objective a farm in keeping with the rural beauty of this specific area. The desire to have this farm yield a profit has been the first consideration. Purchase of the property was partially based upon an appraised timber value in order to evaluate pasture cost so as to keep the investment cost per cow below the locally used break-even figure of $600.00. The work of building fences involved the use of a 1948 Jeep, originally purchased for the Alabama farm, in order to keep down expenses, and a borrowed or rented post-hole auger. My salary since 1961 has ranged between $1.00 and $1.50 per hour, and during periods when I was involved with several tasks, I was required to keep accounts of my time in divisions of capital improvement and operational expenses in order to provide for accurate cost records.

The recent audit in which the "basis of the barbed wire fence built in 1966 was reduced because of lack of substantiation" is quite surprising. Substantiation is basically provided if one examines herd growth and the increased ability to retain calves to a higher weight that this fencing has allowed by gradual pasture improvement and the prevention of overgrazing during dry weather. I was involved with the construction of this barbed wire fencing, specifically two east-west lines, and located this fence in accordance with the plan of the local U.S.D.A. Soil Conservation Service office.

Another section of fencing disallowed under the audit was built around and through a section of woods during the summer of 1966. This was done to provide a shelter (all seasons) area for the cattle, to confine them near the feeding area in the barn during the winter, and to prevent damage to the major portion of the woods by the cattle. All of this fencing was built with barbed wire and is characterized by careful construction (horizontal and vertical alignment) to provide a strong low maintenance fence. The fencing in the woods is very similar to another section of fencing I helped construct along the northwestern woods which was allowed under the 1965 audit.

There is a similar situation in regard to the wooden fencing near the barn. This was allowed under the 1965 audit. This fencing not only provides for the appearance mentioned earlier, but for an emergency holding area for sick cattle, calf weaning and stock storage before and after transport.

One additional item which is worthy of rebuttal is about the application of lime to the pastures for soil pH adjustment. This has been contested as an expense for cattle, yet to my knowledge only one of the horses, which is periodically ridden in this large area to count and move the cattle, has ever been in this area where the contested lime was applied and fencing done.

The careful planning and the construction that has been done has been advantageous to the operation and the operational expense of the farm as my father is now able to handle the majority of the work by working mostly evenings and weekends with only occasional help from a local laborer.

Under penalties of perjury, I declare that this statement to the best of my knowledge and belief is true, correct and complete.

Sincerely,
Fred J. Whitely

123 Diamond Street
Pomona, Midamerica
March 16, 1970

Mr. John B. Nice
Appellate Conferee
Internal Revenue Service

Dear Mr. Nice:

In June 1965, Doctor Roger Whitely visited our office and requested assistance in developing a conservation plan for a farm he had recently purchased in this county.

He made application at this time to become a cooperator with the Soil and Water Conservation District and was accepted by the District Board of Supervisors.

In December of 1965, I walked over the farm with Doctor Whitely and discussed the soils and conservation practices that were needed on his farm. A conservation plan was prepared as a result of this meeting and discussion. The plan was developed with the idea that this would be a beef cow herd type of operation with the farm eventually being all in grass except for woodland. A fencing arrangement was planned to permit rotation of pastures for better management and higher yields. Internal fencing was also suggested to keep the cattle out of the woodland for better management of woodland and continued production.

The plan also included the construction of a farm pond for livestock water for better utilization of pasture land by cattle. Also included were pasture seeding, fertility program before seeding and a fertility program for maintenance. The plan also indicated that when all the conservation practices were applied, this farm could support approximately 50 head of beef cows.

The district has provided technical assistance to him in several instances, for the construction of a livestock pond, pasture seeding, woodland management and the marking of specific, mature trees for harvesting or to be utilized as lumber on the farm.

In my opinion, from the conservation standpoint, Dr. Whitely's farm has been vastly improved since he purchased it. Most conservation practices included in the conservation plan have been applied.

Under penalty of perjury, I declare that this statement to the best of my knowledge and belief is true, correct, and complete.

Respectfully,
Richard Leinhart
District Conservationist

66 Crowley Blvd.
Pomona, Midamerica
March 23, 1970

Mr. John B. Nice
Appellate Conferee
Internal Revenue Service

Sir:

I met Dr. Whitely shortly after he moved here in 1963. Our interest in each other developed because he is a biologist (major—medicine) and mine is biology (general—teaching). He had a cow-calf farm in Alabama running at the time. I had and have a cow-calf program locally. Parenthetically, it is one of the largest in the state. He visited my farm many times between 1963 and 1965. In 1965, he bought a farm and I sold him cows. You will note that these discussions on cattle covered an approximate period of two years prior to him starting a business. To my recollection, we never discussed horses, except that he chided me during my first round-up for him for exhausting myself and daughter by doing this work on foot. He indicated to me he had bought a horse for this and was stabling it at the time at a local rental stable.

It is not conceivable to me that he would have understudied me for two years for hobby purposes. Further, the way he and I operate, with minimal help it is not a pleasure in itself except that satisfaction that we derive from physical labor, productivity and conducting a side business which is related to our primary educational backgrounds.

As we talked about the business aspects, I emphasized to him that one can make a profit if the capital expenditures per cow were kept below $600–$700 and the running expenses kept low by doing the labor maximally by self and family help.

In 1968, he was capitalized to about $26,000. That which is new is only what he had to construct—barn, pens and fencing. Everthing else he has is used equip-

88

ment. He was up to about 36 brood cows in 1968 and has at least the "equivalence" of another 15–20 cows in the diversion program income. The mathematics then become $26,000 plus about $1,000 interest (on pasture land investment) divided by 50 for a sum of $540 per cow.

I have delivered cows to him three times. He has a small pasture of about two acres on the southwest corner of his property. This surrounds the barn. *At each delivery* the cows were dropped into this pasture and *separated from* the rest of the herd or farm. This is a sensible way to quiet them down, get them used to their new surroundings and to observe for adverse habits. A sensible thing that he did was to surround this pasture with a high wooden fencing. The cows are locked in well and I can tell you better than with a wire fence.

His barn is unique. I have been in it many times and admire its construction and planning. I have worked in it with hay. I have watched him feed his cows in it and treat sick cows and calves in it. For the first several years there was no shed. There was just the cow-barn proper. The horses have a couple hundred square feet under a part of the hayloft. I suspect that your auditor drove past the front of the barn along the road and got an erroneous impression. I suspect further that since the farm is both neat and attractive as compared to most cattle farms, it is immediately suspect. This pleasantness should not be taken to imply that there is present a costly frivolous venture. In my opinion, a 40,000 cubic foot barn for $5,150.00 must have taken a lot of work to plan and erect in the latter part of the last decade.

Finally, when I delivered the first cows, the small front pasture was divided into two sections. There was no paddock.

Under penalty of perjury, I declare the statements above are true and accurate to the best of my knowledge.

Very truly yours,
Frank Honor

2345 Canew Street
Pomona, Midamerica
March 5, 1970

Mr. John B. Nice
Internal Revenue Service
Appellate Conferee

Dear Mr. Nice:

In 1965 and 1966 in my capacity as County Extension Agent for Baker County I was in conference with Roger Whitely, M.D. many times both in my office and on his farm. Our planning was for a beef cattle operation in French Township. A soil test sent to State University indicated a need for lime. This was spread with a truck by Robert Agri as agricultural lime using 251,900 pounds to correct the pH of the soil to increase legume growth in the pasture mixture for cattle only. Legume pasture is not good for horses. To increase the existing pasture a fertilizer application was recommended and the Joy Company applied a 15–5–5, a high nitrogen mixture, to stimulate earlier and more growth to carry the cattle already on the farm. I was involved in pasture seedings, using the plow on some fields and an offset disk on others. I know of the stock water pond designed by the district conservationist, the layout of the fields and the cruising of the woodland. This cruising helped to determine the location of cross fences to give winter protection in the edge of the woods for cattle. I knew of the barn location and design for winter feed storage for the cattle. At no time in the planning of this operation were provisions discussed for horses. There is no pasture planted for them and no satisfactory hay fields for horses on this farm.

Anyone familiar with this soil in French Township would realize that there are times that the only way to travel over the land is on horseback or walk. Two or three horses and 55–65 cattle seems to me to be a poor ratio for dividing the expenses of this farm on a 50–50 basis. All the horses use is a small portion of the barn.

G. D. Trut
County Agent (retired)

90

State of Midamerica   )
                              ss:
County of Baker   )
    Before me, the undersigned, a Notary Public in and for said County and State, this *9th* day of March, 1970, personally appeared the within named G. D. Trut and acknowledged the execution of the foregoing statement.
    Witness my hand and Notarial Seal.

                        C. Young
                        Notary Public

My Commission expires:
July 28, 1971

                        4995 15th Street
                        Pomona, Midamerica
                        March 25, 1970
Mr. John B. Nice, Appellate Conferee
Internal Revenue Service
Midtown, Midamerica

Dear Mr. Nice:

    Dr. Roger Whitely has brought to my attention the disallowance of many expenses as deductible items for his farm operation for the years of 1966 through 1968. Since I am familiar with the operation of the farm from its inception to the present time, Dr. Whitely asked me to forward comments as to my opinion of the farm operation as a commercial enterprise.
    From the beginning when he was looking for an appropriate and acceptable farm at reasonable costs up to the present time, I have often conferred with him on the various aspects involved in a detailed and large operation of this nature. I have made numerous trips to the farm, both in winter and in summer, and observed the personal work expended by Dr. Whitely and his wife.
    I wish to clearly state that in my opinion and judgment, based upon my personal observations, this farm was conceived, constructed, and operated from a profit standpoint. The entire direction and total operating frame-work and all discussions in which I was in-

volved have been of a profit motivated nature.

It has been my observation that the majority of the work on the farm has been performed by him and his wife. I have helped him in the wintertime to haul hay from the upper most parts of the barn to the feeding racks for the cattle. I have observed him and his wife making daily trips to the farm for the purpose of feeding the cattle and checking on the condition of the cattle. The pastures have been seeded and built up over a period of several years in order to carry the maximum number of cows and calves for the acreage involved. A minimum of equipment, mostly second hand, and the extensive use of barbed wire indicates the "bare-bones" and economical approach. A tremendous amount of labor has been put forth by Dr. Whitely and his wife in building up this farm to what I believe will be a profitable operation. By the very nature of the farm itself, the building up of the pastures, the building up of the herd, the adding of fences, profits must reasonably be deferred for the first several years.

If I can elaborate further in personal testimony concerning this matter I will be happy to do so.

Yours very truly,
A. G. Virtue
Senior Vice President
First Bank and Trust Co.

State of Midamerica)

       ss.

County of Baker)

On the 25th day of March, 1970, A. G. Virtue, Senior Vice President of the First Bank and Trust Company, Pomona, Midamerica, personally appeared before me, a Notary Public in and for the state and county above mentioned, and personally signed the above document.

May Love
Notary Public

My Commission Expires November 23, 1972

Isn't this a fine assist? If you are going to get a letter as an affidavit from a friend regarding economics, make sure it is like the above one and not like this following short story. *A psychiatrist and a proctologist became good friends and agreed to share office expenses. To economize even further, they had just one sign printed:*

Dr. Marvin Hornstein, Psychiatrist
Dr. David Slodnick, Proctologist
SPECIALIZING IN ODDS AND ENDS[8]

Route 8
Skidmore, Midamerica
March 15, 1970

Mr. John B. Nice
Appellate Conferee
Internal Revenue Service

Dear Mr. Nice:

I have been a laborer on the farm of Dr. Roger Whitely since he bought it in 1965.

I have had only a few years of schooling so Dr. Whitely has helped me with this letter.

Mostly, we work together on Sundays because I have been employed elsewhere during the week. Sometimes we work together on a Saturday afternoon if he is in a push to get something done. 90% to 95% of the time he is with me whether we work 8 hours or 12 hours. He is there to tell me what to do and he helps me with what I do whether it is spreading manure or stringing wire or digging post holes or changing cattle from one pasture to another or repairing fence or taking trees which have fallen down off the fence line or burying dead calves and even once a dead cow. Once in a while he leaves me because he had a call to go back to the hospital or has me started on something that I can do by myself without instruction or without help. These times are rare.

93

Sometime in 1969, a woman called me at my house in Skidmore and asked me some questions. First I thought it must be his secretary but the questions were funny since she asked me what I do on the farm. It is a little hard for me to remember all the questions and what I said but I remember about the manure.

In the spring when we can get a truck into the fields or later on when we had a manure spreader, we work for a month of Sundays to get the cow manure and horse manure spread on the fields. This is what I meant by manure. The amount of manure that is collected by spring is enormous. We used to take it out of the barn by hand but lately when he bought a second-hand tractor with a loader and also the second-hand manure spreader, it is easier. We used to load it in a four wheel Dodge truck and I would stand in the body of the truck and pitchfork it out. Only a four wheel drive truck would have been able to do this early in the spring.

Dr. Whitely has shown me each entry made by the woman he calls an auditor on pages 34, 40, 41, 46, 47, 48, 49, 50, and 51 in the audit. In each instance when my name appears on these pages, she has entered half of my pay under cattle and the other half under horses. The doctor says to use decent language so I will call this a total misrepresentation of the facts.

He is absolutely firm about the horses. His wife and daughter are required to do that work related to them and their stalls. I have never curried their horses. I have never cleaned their hooves. I have never put them in a stall, taken them out of stalls, put a blanket or saddle on them. I have never exercised them. I have never dried them. I have never even touched one of them except by accident.

It is almost five years now I worked on that farm either directly for Dr. Whitely or for his carpenter. One time, repeat, one time, I filled a hole in the stall made by his daughter's horse. Three times, maybe four times I have rolled a wheelbarrow of horse manure out of a stall. I do this in my lunch hour and it is little enough to do for Mrs. Whitely who comes all the way out to feed him and me lunch. I did this for her and only when their daughter is not there to help. Twice I helped unload straw from the truck on Sundays if Mrs. Whitely is able to find it on Sunday. The only other handling of straw is when we take some of the women's straw, usually when they are not around, and make a bed for a sick cow or calf or early in the winter put straw on the ground the day before the cows get into the barn for winter feeding. Once or twice when the women have stuck the straw bales where it gets into the way and Dr. Whitely gets mad, we both move it where it won't interfere.

The horse manure is stacked by the women. By the end of the winter, it is usually mixed with the cow manure. This is the manure which we haul out in the fields to fertilize them. This is what I would have told the lady who called me if I could have had time to think and if the questions she asked would have let me tell the story like it is.

If the doctor has the Sunday's work all planned then when we reach the farm, I go into the tool shed and get the tools out he tells me to on the way there in the truck. Sometimes, if he hasn't figured out which tools we need or what we will do first, he feeds the horses and I get one to three buckets of water and put it in the stall buckets. This takes me one to three minutes out of a usually 600 minute day.

The only other time I was in a stall was when the lofts under which the stalls were made had to be strengthened and I helped the carpenter raise the 6×6 beams in place. I don't remember if the carpenter paid me or Dr. Whitely.

The water we catch off the barn roof. For some reason, Dr. Whitely does not yet have a well. We don't even have a light at the entrance. When we leave in the dark, he puts the truck lights on so I can see my way to the gate. The he drives to the gate to pick me up. He figures these frostings on the cake can wait until the farm pays its own way. He tells me we will dig a well this year. We will probably pound it in ourselves with the pulley that fits on the power take-off on

the back of his farm jeep. He doesn't hire much help,
for what he can do himself or with me.

Under the penalty of perjury, I declare I have
examined this statement and to the best of my knowledge, I believe it is true and accurate.

Very truly yours,
Oscar Fathful

Ernest G. Peed
Forestry Consultant
Rural Route 5, Box 666
North Bristol, Midamerica
May 27, 1965

Dr. Whitely
5000 15th Street
Pomona, Midamerica

Dear Dr. Whitely:

Enclosed please find a table showing the estimated
volume and value of timber on a property located in the
NE 1/4, Sec 70. T20 N, R 6E, in French Township,
Baker County, Midamerica. The tables show both total
volume and value and per acre volume and value. I ex-
tend the value estimate to 15 years at 3% compounded
annually. The timber is probably growing at 6–8% but I
reduced the figure to take into account mortality, wind
damage, etc., and a cut of older trees at sometime within
this 15 years. When a cut is made it will be replaced by
reproduction of pole size trees which will have no
measurable volume for a time. This qualifies a reduction to net value increase during this time.

It has been a pleasure serving you. If I can be of
further assistance please feel free to call.

Sincerely yours,
Ernest G. Peed

Table showing Total Volume, Bd. ft. (Doyle)
and Value of Timber Stand.

	Total Vol.	Value	Value/acre	Total Value at 15 yrs. @ 3%
Veneer	41350	$3,167.75	$216.32	
Common	95972	2,936.18	157.11	
Totals		$6,103.93	$373.43	$9,510.92

Cruise made for Dr. Whitely, 5000 15th Street, Pomona, Midamerica on May 26, 1965 by Ernest G. Peed, Forestry Consultant.

NOBLE FARM SERVICE
Richard Noble
22 Hedge Row
Pomona, Midamerica
March 8, 1970

Mr. John B. Nice
Appellate Conferee
Appellate Division
Internal Revenue Service
Midtown, Midamerica

Dear Sir:

This statement or affidavit is in regard to questions asked of me by Dr. Roger Whitely. He stated simply that there were questions as to his motives in purchasing and operating his farm in French Township.

In 1965, I was the Vice President and Farm Manager of the First Bank and Trust Co., Pomona, Midamerica. As such, I appraised a farm for mortgage loan purposes in French Township for him. He subsequently purchased this farm and we supplied the loan funds.

Dr. Whitely had previously owned a cattle farm in Alabama, as well as forest lands. He evidently knew a fair amount about these matters as it turned out in our discussions. He finally decided to buy this particular farm based upon my appraisal of the value of the open acreage, and his personal as well as a timber expert's opinion after cruise of the forest land. He realized that the open land was less acreage than he desired but the total package was as good as he could find in the two year search he had conducted with my help.

There was nothing in our talks at the time which would have caused me to think that he did not have a profit motive in mind for a cow-calf operation. He knew from my advice on this farm, as well as others I had appraised for him, that it would be a good three years before northern pastures would be well developed on what had previously been a grain farm; this farm had no improvements whatsoever on it. This delay period had to be well known, and is common knowledge to farmers and farm managers; it would not be reasonable to expect a cash profit before the fourth year given these common circumstances.

When it became evident to him that the potential profits could be increased with more land, since the barn and equipment base had been established, he again sought my aid in 1969 as a private farm manager and consultant in attempting to acquire further acreage contiguous with his present holdings. We were, however unsuccessful at a price consistent with a cow-calf operation. A major problem is that nearby land, relatively unproductive at present, is nonetheless profitable to the owners through participation in the Feed Grain Program and its subsidy payments.

Knowing Dr. Whitely, his abilities and knowledge of the beef situation and what he has done through the years audited (as well as in 1969) I do not understand the IRS statement: "Farm experts (unidentified) in this area have stated that there is no possibility for a profit with an operation of this size. A profit motive has not been substantiated and personal motives are dominant."

The question arises as to whether the quoted farm experts were really discussing profitability, or family income needs. In other words, a given unit may be profitable and yet not capable of supporting an operator if the farm income be the sole source of family support. I would wonder if the auditor has been asked the basis on which it was established that personal motives were dominant.

As I know the farm, I am certain that it could show a profit if nothing is done to it except to participate in the Feed Grain Program. Or, Dr. Whitely could show a substantial profit by simply selling the farm. He does advise me that his fourth full year of production on the farm does show a profit.

It would seem to the undersigned that it is indeed his intent to operate his farm for profit; it would also seem that it is on the verge of doing so.

Respectfully submitted,
Richard Noble

State of Midamerica)
        ss.
County of Baker)

Before me, the undersigned, a Notary Public in and for said County and State, this *8th* day of March, 1970, personally appeared the within named Richard Noble and acknowledged the execution of the foregoing statement.

Witness my hand and Notarial Seal.

G.E. Cryoler, Notary Public

My commission expires:
27 June, 1973

Are you beginning to perceive any difference between those who vouch for our operation and those initiating and continuing this absurd "audit"?

The barn is so constructed that at any time, I can convert it with ease so that 1/3 of it may be used for 8 brood mares (which I am thinking of doing now since my farm is quarantined with Bang's disease of the cattle). It is known to me that I can make this conversion and still carry on a larger brood cow program with a loss of simply a relatively small hay storage area.

It is known to me that I do not feel any twinge of

99

immorality when I put gas in my 1949 farm Universal Jeep fully depreciated with IRS approval of all such entries (Xerox copy of all IRS forms for all of those years available on your request). It is also known to me that I do not feel any twinge of immorality when, instead of gas, I put that fuel designated as hay into my farm horse. (See 4 of preceding testimonies about farm horse.)

In regard to the way I have kept my farm books, it is known to me that I have never been previously penalized. I will have them for you.

A good man can be stupid and still be good. But, a bad man must have brains—absolutely.[9]

It is known to me that all of these inconsistencies resulted in an audit multiple scores of pages long in regard to a relatively small business.

The number of entries made by the auditor calls to mind the discussion between two women: *First woman: "Did you hear about Mrs. Gaffney having quadruplets? I understand that this happens only once every 60,000 times." Second woman: "Glory be! When does she get her housework done?"*[10]

It is known to me that several interviewees consider that this audit is of harassment type.

Of all the tyrannies on humankind, the worst is that which persecutes the mind.[11] *Dictators ride to and fro upon tigers from which they dare not dismount.*[12] *I believe that there are more instances of the abridgement of the freedom of the people by gradual and silent encroachments of those in power than by violent and sudden usurpations.*[13] *The most insupportable of tyrannies is that of inferiors.*[14] *There is a cowardly propensity in the human heart that delights in op-*

pressing somebody else, and in the gratification of this base desire we always select a victim that can be outraged with safety.[15]

When my request for an experienced auditor, so that this one should not drag out for 17 months as did the immediately previous one, could not be handled by the local office and after it was forwarded to group supervisor New C. Ants, he stated in a letter dated February 12, 1969, "The Internal Revenue Service sets very high standards for the selection of its agents and they receive intensive training after they are selected both in class-room courses and on-the-job-training." It is known to me that as Chairman and Professor of a Department of the Medical College of the South, it was my administrative function to relieve of her duties a registered technologist for incompetence and during a period that I allowed her pay and work in the department while she was looking for another position but assigned her to simple aide duties, she was taking some sort of correspondence course related to income taxes. (At this stage of writing, April 10, two affidavits related to this have not yet been received. My southern investigative agency has not apparently completed its work. If the material arrives before April 23, I will fetch them to you. They will be numbered 45 and 46.) The parallelism here is that I would not let the pseudo-technologist anywhere near a complicated machine no more than the assigner of duties should have placed Mrs. N. Olittle in a position to audit these accounts. I have indicated to Messrs. Cicada, Crackpot and Ants that the auditor was charming, gracious and conscientious but I continue to voice objection to any management system which places an employee in a situation potentially embarrassing and damaging because experience gained on the job is not yet sufficient.

Most vices may be committed very genteely: A man may

debauch his friend's wife genteely; he may cheat at cards genteely.[16]

That Blondie's experience was inadequate is not only confirmed by the character of the audit but by the fact that at both meetings she was accompanied by a man who must have been assigned a supportive role. We have mentioned his great contributions—asking for gas bills and saying the farm was too small. Mrs N. Olittle then parroted this latter, like a good student, into audit statements. My experts refute her unidentified "farm experts," herself and her hand-holder.

Now hear from one of my experts, another man of the cloth.

DOUBLE 'A' RANCH
REG. POLLED HEREFORDS
Box 000 Chreisburg
Midamerica
March 10, 1970

Mr. John B. Nice
Appellate Conferee
Internal Revenue Service

Dear Mr. Nice:

I have a farm 1/2 mile from Dr. Roger Whitely in Baker County. This farm is smaller than his and we have made some money on it. We have a cow-calf program on it of Reg. Polled Herefords.

My sons and I make hay for the doctor from his fields.

In 1967, we made no hay but cut a field with a rotary mower for weed control. This was his middle field and that year had just been planted.

In 1968, we cut a southeast pasture and a small pasture around the barn including grass in the paddock. The oval fencing around the paddock did not interfere

102

with the cutting. We made 876 bales from these fields.

By 1969, we were able to make 1205 bales of hay from one field on one cutting. The quantity would have been greater but the cut hay was rained upon. Despite the fact that over 1200 bales of hay were taken from this land in the year, he was still grazing his herd on this same pasture until Dec. 21 when it became covered with snow. This shows that the pastures are progressively becoming more productive and now in the fourth year are effectively reducing the amount of hay he had to purchase elsewhere.

I quote the auditor "the calf crop from the breeding cattle is the only crop."

My only "crop" is from breeding cows, and I do not think I am doing something wrong.

Under penalty of perjury, I declare I have examined this statement and to the best of my knowledge and belief it is true and correct.

Signed:
Oner Alwas

Mr. New C. Ants' statement of 2-12-69 does not coincide with the facts of life.

It is known to me that not even group supervisor Mr. Ants and District Director Dandy use the same field manuals from which to obtain guidelines. (My use of the term "field manuals" is derived from a portion of twenty years of my life which I devoted to my country as a reserve officer in its army.) In one instance Ants says I can gain affidavits, by permission from Dandy, from various auditors. Imagine taxpayers' surprise when Dandy says no!

Certainly, the taxpayers are struggling with a wraith.

If you read the correspondence with Ants, notice his confusion as to where my case had passed.

These incongruities are beyond my comprehension.

Myself, when young, did eagerly frequent Doctor and

Saint and heard great argument about it and about, but evermore came out by the same door I went in.[17]

I ask in the argumentative form permitted by you to me, how can Mr. Ants or any other responsible person declare an employee of sufficient competence who puts a purchased item such as seven neck chains for the identification of cattle in an auditing column which is marked indeterminate and must mean she does not know whether they are for cattle or horses or vehicles and who for months allows no expense for purchased crushed corn and steer fattener and claims that their use is indeterminate to her. The auditor apparently called Grain Marketing, Inc. of Pomona to find out the potential use of $2.55 worth of omolene. I ask a question that I think is reasonable: if she did not want to bother me, as she also stated to my wife, and if she did not want to inquire of cotaxpayer, spouse, about such a weightless item as each 1/2 ton of grain, then why when she was questioning people did she stop with $2.55 worth of omolene, or whatever its price and not question the grain division of the same facility about a ton and a half of food for cows. I did not eat it; my patients did not eat it; the horses did not eat it. You are hereby supplied an answer which she could have readily obtained.

GRAIN MARKETING ASSOCIATION, INC.
First Street
Pomona, Midamerica
March 31, 1970

Mr. J. B. Nice
Appellate Conferee
Internal Revenue Service

Dear Mr. Nice:

Were I to be asked whether a feed mixture of 700

lbs. of crushed corn, 200 lbs. of ground cobs, 100 lbs. of steer fattener, 4 lbs. of salt and 1 lb. of Vitamin A or a mixture containing 900 lbs. of crushed corn, 100 lbs. of steer fattener, 4 lbs. of salt and 1 lb. of Vitamin A was a cattle or horse food mixture, I would respond it was a mixture planned for cattle.

Under penalty of perjury, I declare the statement above is true and accurate to the best of my knowledge.

Very truly yours,
O. N. Pedistil, General Manager
Grain Marketing Assn., Inc.

I am for a change in concurrence with Mr. Joseph Kraft.[18] Editorializing about the postal strike, he says, "At the core there were the same feelings that have inspired indignant protests from Negroes, young people, commuters, stockholders, consumers, and millions of other Americans. There was the sense of impotence—of absolute helplessness in the face of institutions made impervious to ordinary people by size, bureaucratic structure, and mechanized routine," and I am also in concurrence with him when he says, "But there is a far larger more difficult question at stake. There is the question of how to deal with the sense of impotence, of not being able to make grievances known, that affect so many people in all walks of life and then causes such grave disorders." Actually, as I analyze what I am attempting to do here with this story is to make grievances known and also to hope that you have sufficient influence to carry them further.

Sir, I protest not only the audit but the penalties for the bookkeeping. Certainly after her revising them, the end result is not only poor but chaotic. Why does my family separate gasoline accounts if not for purposes of proper journal entries? Is it the intent of these inspections to discourage such a good habit? Yes, I am going to let you hear even from the owner of our local service station.

Sincere Service Center, Inc.
U.S. Route X-9 and Desota St.
Pomona, Midamerica
March 16, 1970

Mr. John B. Nice
Appellate Conferee
Internal Revenue Service

Dear Mr. Nice:

Dr. Whitely has shown to me an Internal Revenue letter dated February 19, 1970 and signed by a conferee. He takes exception to the statement in the letter which reads as follows: "I also concur in her proposed application of Section 6653 (a) penalties for the manner in which you have kept and maintained your records of your farm operation."

The doctor, Mrs. Whitely and, rather recently, their daughter drive three road vehicles. One is a very old farm universal four-wheel drive jeep; one is a half-ton 4-wheel drive truck and one is the family car.

The systems that we use for paying me are as follows: a credit card is used for the automobile; for the trucks, originally a cash slip was handed to him at the time of each purchase. For the past several years to reduce his journal entries, I issue him by mail a statement for all the indebtedness owed to me for the previous month. He does not now bother to pick up a copy of these cash purchases for the trucks nor for the gas we place in containers for the farm tractor. He is always in a hurry and besides, he trusts me. When he is en route to the University Medical Center at midafternoon once a week but must detour past the farm to feed, he is then in the family car and if it is low on gas he stops here. He just gives me the credit card and drives on. Mrs. Whitely picks it up the next time she comes by.

They seem to use particular care to keep the accounts of the vehicles separated. I do not know what the entries would look like in the books they keep and this is not my business. However, anyone who would go

106

through the formalities cited above must do them for the reason of maintaining accurate records; certainly it would be simpler to use the same credit card.

Under the penalty of perjury, I declare I have examined this statement and to the best of my knowledge, believe it is true and accurate.

Very truly yours,
Abraham Sincere

Why do I double check my accountants via my broker? I assure you it is not simply to burden him at tax time.

Here is his supportive letter. But before you read it, ask yourself and then tell me when we meet, why didn't the auditor, her handholder, her supervisor, the regional conferee—why didn't they check these dozens upon dozens of stock transactions? Were the accountants, the brokerage firm and myself considered so infallible in these non-farm areas, to be incapable of error? No wrong date, such as entering one which would thereby convert a short term gain with a $50+\%$ tax to a long term gain with just a 25% tax? How can this be?

COURAGEOUS AND CO.
333 Olive Street
Pomona, Midamerica
April 1, 1970

Mr. John B. Nice
Internal Revenue Service
Appellate Conferee

Dear Mr. Nice:

The purpose of this letter is to indicate to you my observation of the care Dr. Whitely has exercised in obtaining the information necessary for the reporting of the securities gains and losses experienced through transactions handled by my office. In the years 1966 and 1967, although I understand that he employed pro-

107

fessional help in preparing his federal income tax forms
he asked that I give him a record of capital gains and
losses and dividend income from his securities transactions. It is my understanding that he wished this information from me so that he could cross check his accountants to be sure that the matter was properly handled. He also asked for this same information in 1968
although it is my understanding that he prepared the
tax forms himself.

If I can be of any further assistance on this matter,
I would be most happy to do so.

Very truly yours,
U. P. Wright

Signed this *1st* day of *April,* 1970 in my presence.

Francine Xavier
Notary Public

My commission expires June 4, 1970

Why do spouse and I separate horse and cattle veterinary bills, both of supply type and professional service type? Surely you will not consider this an exercise
for exercise itself.

MASON'S VETERINARY HOSPITAL
600 Maine Avenue
Pomona, Midamerica
March 16, 1970

Mr John B. Nice
Appellate Division Conferee
Internal Revenue Service

Dear Mr. Nice:

I have been and still am the Veterinarian for the
farm of Dr. and Mrs. Roger Whitely in Baker County,
Midamerica. There are no entries made in the audit for
the years 1966, 1967 and 1968 in reference to another
one. That is, if they have paid for any other advice, it
could not have been expensed as tax-deductible since
the auditor does not show such in her 52 page thesis.

Of the scores of purchases or visits that are shown in the audit as relating to my business, she has placed everything under "cattle," as was correct, with two exceptions.

In 1966, just after the horses were moved to the farm, there is an expense of $8.00 which I charged as "worm horses," on March 14, 1966. This was paid for in cash. On this invoice you will note that the doctor or his representative has written "1/2 farm." In his journal you will note under same date an entry of $4.00 in his column labeled "Veterinary, Medicine and Livestock supplies." These headings are in a record book prepared by the Department of Agricultural Economics, State University. I am not attesting as to whether four dollars of the total medicine was used for a horse which I claim is a farm horse or the same horse that you may claim is not a farm horse. I do not state what its use is. I state that Dr. Whitely considered it to be a farm horse and kept a record of the transaction and further, I state that is it evident that the remaining four dollars was not declared by him to be a deductible expense since the money was not expensed but obviously paid out of personal accounts. This half of the medicine could have been used for the pet horse of his daughter, or indeed thrown away. I conclude that the tax-payer realizes that worming a pet is not a farm expense.

In the next *31 months* the auditor cannot find any other contestable veterinary items despite their numbers until Oct. 10, 1968. The reason for this is that his wife pays me separately for horses, whether they be farm or nonfarm type. On that date, my office issued a voucher labeled "med" in the amount of $3.00 cash. The auditor placed it in an audit column headed "?". On the bottom of this voucher there is written, presumably by the doctor or his bookkeeper the word "posted." The farm journal indicates that this $3.00 item was entered in his books under a column labeled: "Misc., Vet, Commissions, Ads." It is a fact that it is unreasonable to believe that after 31 months of uncontestable entries Dr. Whitely would then deliberately enter a $3.00 personal item to be expensed as tax deductible. I am sorry that my office was not more specific about this entry. I cannot recall what it was. On the basis of my four and 1/2 years experience with this farm and the time or season of the year, I would think that he was restocking his scour tablets or antibiotics and needed it in a hurry because you will note on same voucher that spouse taxpayer had to come to my office for it.

He keeps a supply of medicine in his refrigerator at the farm. This is known to me since I not only see it there, but I use it from there. Some types of medicine *must* be refrigerated or otherwise kept cool. It is a fact that I wish I had a refrigerator which would run a whole year for some unknown amount *less* than $6.76 in 1966, $7.90 in 1967 and $7.51 in 1968 which were the *total* amounts allowed on the farm for all electricity. These figures are known to me since they have been pointed out to me in the IRS audit sheets.

Under the penalty of perjury, I declare that I have examined this statement and to the best of my knowledge, I believe that it is true and accurate.

Sincerely,
Dr. Theodore Pure, D.V.M.

Truly, how infantile can an audit get when it declares that the summer work of two engineers who just finished college, both paid thrifty wages by me, $1.25–$1.50 per hour, who labored hard to accomplish and complete the plans of federal and county agents by dividing one field into three pastures was not totally for cattle? That instead, the miles of barbed wire they stretched and erected was barbed wire for the protection of horses and "show horses" no less, which "show horses" we like to leave run through hill and vale still unfenced, by audit definition, over the whole place. Notice her fancy bookkeeping in which, whereas I have properly divided their labors into general and capital type she blithely takes out of my capital expenditure column and places them in a general expense category. I sure wish I could do this!

What does the second engineer who put up these

110

barbed wire "show horse" corrals have to say?

1200 Park Lane
Hamilton, North Dakota
March 15, 1970

Mr. John B. Nice
Appellate Conferee
Internal Revenue Service

Sir:

During the summer of 1966, I was employed on the cattle farm of Dr. Roger Whitely which is situated in French Township, Baker County.

The purpose of my employment was to construct two (2) east-west internal fence lines to divide 90 acres of pasture into three (3) fields and fence around and through a small wooded area. These fences were built in accordance with a plan provided by the District Soil Conservation Office.

The division of the pasture area was to provide a field rotation capability for cattle during grazing seasons and to provide for gradual improvements of the pastures. The fence in the woods was built to provide a shelter area during the summer and protection against cold during the winter. I also built a windbreak in this wooded area which is close to the feeding troughs in the barn. The fences were built with barbed wire and wood posts which were suitably spaced for enclosing cattle pastures.

Taking into consideration the barbed wire fences, the rough character of the wooded area and the plan for field rotation, there is no doubt that I was working to improve a cattle farm. This statement is further substantiated by the fact that there were a number of cattle grazing on the land the entire summer of 1966.

Under penalty of perjury, I declare that these statements are true, correct and complete to the best of my knowledge.

David Larry, II

Witness:
Sworn to and before me this *16th* day of March, 1970.
Notary public for the state of North Dakota

Geneva Thompson

My commission expires 11–14–73

And now heed you the language used by a professional trainer about "show horses" and where they are stabled and a little more about the "show horse" training ring.

BARREN HILL STABLE
Rural Route 10
Pomona, Midamerica
February 18, 1970

Mr. John B. Nice
Appellate Conferee
Internal Revenue Service

Dear Mr. Nice:

I will continue about a third horse.

In the spring of 1967, we recommended the purchase of a better horse for their daughter. We did select a show prospect—a mare of good blood lines which could be used by them as a brood mare if she did not qualify as a show horse. Such a mare was purchased from Saddle Farms in Gibralter, Midamerica for the price of $3,500.00. This horse was moved directly to our stables and she was under my training until October 1, 1967. At that date she was moved to the Whitely farm for cheaper winter keep. On April 1, 1968 this horse was returned to me for continued training. After two seasons of training it was decided to make a brood mare out of her. She was returned to their farm and in the spring of 1969 was shipped out to be bred.

These then, are the auditor's "show horses." At no time has there been any professional training at their farm. There is no actual training ring there. The paddock they have enclosed was built for their daughter's safety and restriction. It is not banked. It is not flat. It is just a piece of rolling pasture. It was not put in the first year. It is an incident to the farm and not a purpose of the farm, as I see it.

Under the penalty of perjury, I declare that I have examined this statement and to the best of my knowledge, I believe it to be true and accurate.

Very truly yours,
A. S. Expert

Let us take any year and look at this pleasure horse farm. Whom did we pay to feed the horses? Where are such entries expressed in my books? Whom did we pay to clean up their manure? Where are the day in and day out labor expenses for feeding the cattle during the winter and caring for them in the spring, summer and fall? Who is mowing the weeds that are still appearing in these relatively young pastures?

Consider how the lilies grow in the fields; they do not work, they do not spin; and yet, I tell you, even Solomon in all his splendor was not attired like one of these.[19]

Are there other than spouse and daughter and myself on a constant daily basis? I will have my *good* books with me when we meet. Please ask yourself, how can the labor bill be so small? Who really did the work? Was it Mr. Fathful who comes some Sundays from Skidmore, twenty miles distant? Does he sneak up at night for a round trip of 40 miles to feed the horses? By the way, Mr. Fathful is afraid of horses!

Let us look at a little more really fancy bookkeeping a la IRS. What ate in 1966 the 1,395 bales of hay plus the approximately 400 bales I had remaining from 1965? Was it the 60 cattle which were not fenced in or was it eaten by the two horses?

I will ask you at the end of this reasonable conference what the horses did with 60,000 pounds of agricultural limestone and I will want to know why a quarter million pounds of lime is a joint expense. I wish to tell my expert, who cannot find any horse grazing pastures for such a quantity of lime nor any fields seeded for hay for the horses. What do horses want with liquid fertilizer spread out on a cow pasture a half mile from their stalls? How would Mrs. N. Olittle and Mr. Crackpot get vendor trucks to the cattle squeeze and barn in the winter if there be no short gravel farm road allowed in the clay country of Midamerica?

Please note that the veterinarian is envious of my allowable electricity bill. The grand total for the three years permitted for me, a doctor, is $22.17. I am advised that I am a good manager, but shades (rather, let there be light) of Thomas Edison, I do not wish my fame to rest on this remarkable feat. Such thrift would require my bust in some Hall of Fame.

In 1965, my expenses on this Midamerica farm were $4,249.71. Is it possible for someone in the IRS to retroactively reprimand auditor Phil Mein and conferee Crackpot for significant dereliction of duty by finding NOTHING improper in those superb books?

It can be proved, but I did not suggest that this go into the applicable affidavit, that one of our vendors, a fulltime farmer, is the son of a man who was killed on this farm doing custom plowing. He was breaking up my very first field. If this be a pleasure farm in the eye of the decedent's son, will someone please explain to me why he purchases my calves and sells us hay, even though he knows that by my mere ownership I have some culpability in reference to the death of his father?

Who is so capable of stretching his imagination to conclude that Blondie is correct in her method of depreciating cattle? I can find only conferee Crackpot. The two mere professional accounting firms are in disagreement with these members of the IRS. Read from them; do not read only the embryonic auditor's audit!

A.B. CADE & COMPANY

Certified Public Accountants
Honeysuckle, Alabama
April 3, 1970

Mr. John B. Nice
Appellate Conferee
Internal Revenue Service

Re: Dr. Roger Whitely
Pomona, Midamerica

Dear Mr. Nice:

Several years ago, Dr. Roger Whitely was associated with the Medical College in Plantation, Alabama, and we prepared his income tax returns. We prepared these for several years and the last year was for 1965.

During the time he was our client, he acquired an operating farm near Honeysuckle. From information supplied by him, we prepared the returns and this would have included setting up depreciable assets. We understand that some difference of opinion has developed concerning the farm assets and lives used.

Based on information that we have been provided, we understand that specifically an auditor of the Internal Revenue Service has proposed that a cow costing $113.00 should have a salvage of $100.00 assigned to it and the balance of $13.00 be depreciated over an eight year period.

This firm is in its 43rd year and I have been associated with it for 17 years and am presently senior partner. I have been certified for more than 20 years, am a member of the Bar and was associated with the Internal Revenue Service as an agent and special agent for 4 years prior to returning to public accounting in 1953. Though Honeysuckle is not a farming community, and though we do not pretend to be specialists in farming, we do auditing and tax work for a number of farm operations in this area, including a 22,000 acre ranch which is reputed to be the largest working ranch east of the Mississippi.

115

In my experience, I have never heard of such a treatment of depreciation of livestock as your auditor proposed. In fact, to my knowledge, I do not recall ever seeing salvage value assigned to livestock on a tax return in this area. It was and would still be our opinion that a cow which cost $113.00 (if, in fact, a "cow") would either already be old or sick or undesirable and, in fact, probably should not be assigned a life as long as 8 years and would therefore, have little or no residual value.

Although we have written this letter at the request of Dr. Whitely, the opinions are ours and we have no interest in his case nor do we expect to be compensated for writing the letter.

It is our understanding that, as an enrolled attorney, it is not necessary that this statement be in affidavit form but simply to state it is true to the best of my knowledge and belief and is based on facts I either know to be true or which I believe to be true, is sufficient attestation.

Yours very truly,
A.B. CADE & COMPANY
Rudolph Proper

Cliffdweller and Kucher
Certified Public Accountants
Real Road
Pomona, Midamerica
April 3, 1970

Re: Roger and Sarah Whitely
Social Security #000-000-0000
Statement Regarding Internal Revenue Examination

Form 1040 for Calendar Years 1966, 1967 and 1968

The above named taxpayers have requested me to comment on an aspect of the current revenue agent's examination. The area of concern is the establishment of a fair salvage value for breeding livestock. It has been my experience in similar situations that the sal-

116

vage value at the end of the realistic useful life of breeding stock is negligible. Since this is not a material factor in the determination of taxable income, it is generally not considered.

I declare under the penalty of perjury that this statement has been examined by me and to the best of my knowledge and belief is a true, correct and complete statement.

George Fineman, CPA
Partner

Let us define audit and then preferably use our own test. "Official examination of claims or accounts." "A balance sheet, result of analyzing and checking an account"[20] I claim that an analysis should be thorough. I claim that an audit should have some semblance of balance. I claim that the facts should be represented in an audit. I further claim that such an analysis should result in a learning experience. What good are audits, or car inspections for that matter, if the audited person does not learn (gain an experience from) the inspection. There must be constancy and there must be consistency. Advise me where I find these when I contrast the 1963 farm audit and the 1964–1965 farm audit with the present "audit."

I cannot allow my learned accounting consultants to be deprecated. Sir, at times someone must say, "No." I am willing to so say a "Resounding No," though this editorial says it better than I.

RESOUNDING NO
Reprinted from Midtown News
April 1, 1970

The current issue of "Private Practice," journal of the Congress of County Medical Societies, has some useful words to say on the current binge of "positivism" in many areas of American life.

The opinions offered by "Private Practice" editor Marvin Henry Edwards are directed specifically to the medical field, where governmental in-

117

trusion and a demand for "positive" co-operation by doctors have reached new levels of intensity. They could be applied as well to a number of other fields where similar intrusions and demands are making themselves apparent.

In his editorial and in an address to the Association of American Dentists, Edwards puts his finger on the overriding fallacy of the so-called "positive" argument: The fact that it allows the proponents of big government, expanded subsidies, and proliferating controls to define what is "positive" and what is not. If you cooperate with the slide into collectivism, you are constructive; if you don't cooperate, you are negative.

What really needs discussing in all such cases, Edwards observes, is the matter of the ultimate goal and the effect of the trend in question. If government control of the medical profession means loss of freedom for doctor and patient, greater cost, and inferior service, there is in fact nothing "positive" about going along with it. The right course is to resist such programs altogether.

Edwards notes in this respect that Medicine has been showing some very distinct suicidal tendencies. The question has not been: Should we help the government operate its health planning schemes, or should we help the government impose new controls upon us? The only question has been: How? To this approach he proposes the simple alternative—the most truly "positive" course of all—of saying "No" to the planners. The same course should be adopted by businessmen and others invited to participate in various Federal schemes.

The great domestic battle of our time is the battle to prevent big government from absorbing the energies and dominating the lives of its private citizens. Any attempt to paint co-operation with this effort as "positive" or "constructive" is merely playing with words. Private citizens can best be positive about the goal of liberty by greet-

ing all efforts at control with a resounding negative.[21]

And still others say it differently but nevertheless suc-
cinctly. *Stand up to the devil and he will turn and run.*[22] *It is
so stupid of modern civilization to have given up believing in
the devil when he is the only explanation of it.*[23]

It is known to me, and to those assisting spouse
and me with testimony submitted before (pages 65, 70,
72, 77, 78, 82, 83, 84, 86, 87, 90, 91, 93, 96, 97, 102,
104, 106, 107, 108, 111, 112, 114, 116) of the personal
work done on this farm by self and family, of profit
motivation, of bare-bones approach, of the deference of
profit for build-up, of the true value of the Alabama
timber, of the flexibility of farm building design, of the
use of the barn, and the high ratio of barn space between cows and horses, of the use of very low cost
lumber, of the repudiation of the IRS claim of the cost
of the wooden fencing, of the separation of costs of vehicle needs, of the repudiation of claims of the auditor's
"farm experts," of the attempts to increase farm size, of
the refutation of the incompatibility of farm size with
profit, of the increased productivity of the farm, of the
need for feeder calves in this area, of the separation of
hay accounts, of the expert federal and state advice so
often used, of the use of a farm horse, of the preponder-
ant use of the barn for business, of the absence of hay
fields for horses, of the true nature of fencing, of the
separation of veterinary bills into cattle and horse com-
ponents, of appropriate bookkeeping, of the ridiculous
allowance for electricity (2¢ per day), of the true nature
of the auditor's show horses and training "ring," of the
true nature, not falsely assumed nature, of the work
performed by my week-end farm hand, of the actual
underpayment of my sons for labor, of the judgment of
others about the quality of this audit, of the true use of
one quarter of a million lbs. of lime, and fertilizer, of
the incompleteness of the audit, of the period of under-
study before investment, of the soil and water conserva-

tion plan followed and, sir, then your reading of these will let the facts be known to you.

For lack of fuel, a fire dies down.[24]

I am upset that a business novice was assigned to me against my original advice, or does not the IRS take good advice, and then who capriciously treated vouchers as fitted her thinking or, as I suspect, the thinking of her advisors, rather than mine, or my accountants, or the number of experts who are testifying for me; that this cavalier treatment has interfered with my rest, with my professional work, has caused a burden on others to refute incorrect statements with facts. It is in part due to this audit that I have resigned my executive position at the hospital.

It should be realized that few men, aside from uncommon men such as am I, will continue (or start) in a small business if all these hardships are induced by the IRS. I, therefore, assure you that I have grave concern for my country and will make every effort, not only in regard to my own situation but for the good of others, that this unfair audit be overthrown.

Where will your family get the beef for its table if each cattle farmer has audits of this type? The 1964 Census of Agriculture by the U.S. Department of Commerce shows, vastly differently from the thinking of the IRS person accompanying Mrs. N. Olittle and differently from the thinking of the "experts" she conceals, that:

Herds of 1–4   head, number —581,401
          5–9   head, number —333,795
          10–19 head, number —436,547
          20–29 head, number —267,513
          30–49 head, number —238,584—my herd is
                                       in this group.

I have said elsewhere that it is of little difference to me where I fight for my country. The IRS cannot intimidate me, for if it can do so to *me,* God save America.

There has been no gain to me from all these tests. I hope to find "reasonable people" as I proceed up the steps with this audit.

Attend to the wording of your own services instructions, paragraph I, Publication 5 (Rev. 1–69) Right of Appeal and Preparing Protests for Unagreed Cases "Reasonable people sometime disagree on tax issues."

Who has been reasonable so far?

I recalled during this preparation an invitation to which I responded by lecturing at the Texas Medical Association meeting in January, 1962. I was one of the many hundreds in attendance at the main speech given by Captain Eddie Rickenbacker. I have today (April 4) received the text of that speech from his secretary via airmail to meet the deadline I had suggested to him. There follow some selected paragraphs.

> 1962 Conference
> Texas Medical Association
> Austin, Texas, January 20, 1962
> "Conservatism Must Face Up to Liberalism"
> by Captain Eddie Rickenbacker
> Chairman of the Board
> Eastern Airlines, Inc.

THE CANCEROUS SIXTEENTH AMENDMENT—PERSONAL INCOME TAX

Fifty years have passed since Woodrow Wilson said that "a concentration of governmental power is what always preceded the death of Human Liberty." When Wilson said that in 1912, governmental power was not concentrated in Washington. It was scattered through all the states of the Union.

Government money means government power and in 1912 most of the government money belonged to the states, counties, cities and towns. These local governments in 1912 spent more than two-thirds of all taxes collected in the United States, while the Federal government controlled and spent less than one-third.

How do we stand today? In 1960, all local and Federal taxes took one-third or 33% of all our earnings, against only nine percent 50 short years ago, and in 1960 the Federal government took, controlled and spent 70 per cent of that 33 percent instead of one-third of nine percent of our earnings as was done 50 short years ago.

Of course, this disastrous increase in Federal taxation has seriously injured every American's power to spend or save what he or she has earned. But there is a deeper and more dangerous injury.

For government money is government power and the federal government today has 65 times as much power to invade the personal liberty of every American citizen as it had in 1912. And it is using that power to an even greater degree.

As a result of this growing Federal power, the American citizen finds himself in almost daily contact with the Federal government. There are 2,500 Federal agencies and they all think the American citizen has nothing better to do than fill out forms. And you better not ignore these or make an error. If you do, Washington will throw the book at you.

I ask you in all seriousness, how can this law be enforced fairly? A man could spend his life trying to learn the tax law and still not know it all. How can we expect 60 or 70 million people to respect a law that cannot be understood?

Isn't it obvious that every tax payer must make some kind of mistake sooner or later? Isn't it obvious that a law so difficult that it must be violated gives the Federal government the power to prosecute just about anybody it sets its sights on? Isn't this the type of power that can and will destroy the last vestige of liberty?

But there is another result of the Federal tax law that is even more dangerous. Under the cancerous Sixteenth—the Income Tax—Amendment, which became effective in 1913, ironically, under President Wilson who had been so concerned about government power—under the Sixteenth Amendment the entire gross income of every American is subject to complete Federal confiscation.

Ladies and gentlemen, we are not yet in bondage. We still have some liberty left. But we are at war to preserve that liberty. Let us, therefore, acknowledge and be grateful for the blessings of freedom, which God has given us. Let us dedicate our lives to this one struggle.[25]

Let us take a few more excerpts from the auditor's 52 pages.

The auditor says that there were three horses kept in the barn in 1966. This is a lie (her page eight).

She says that the expenditures attributable to the cattle were allowed in toto. This is a fabrication, an inconceivable one. Refer to the $10.20 attributed to the cattle from purchases from just one store, out of a total purchase of about $2,000.00. Note however, the absence of any ocular cataract when she adds up the horse purchases at the same outlet. Do you see that she has found 2800% more purchases for horses than for cattle in this same year as identifiable?

How can this be? Will you or SOMEBODY ask her what "A careful evaluation of the farm and farming activities was made" means? When was she on the property? Who unlocked the gate for her? Who gave her authority to invade my privacy by climbing over the white board fencing (in her pregnant state), a fencing she must obviously detest, to evaluate the activities (see photograph). What activities did she see? Did she ever see my wife or myself up to midcalf in stool? I have included the names of my farm experts. Who are hers? What "show horses"? (see photograph). What "training ring"? (her page eleven). What does this sentence standing out as a paragraph unrelated to anything before or after mean: "In 1966 a pond was built that has been stocked for fishing"? I don't follow the context. I cannot find it! The pond was built for water! It is that simple. (See affidavits.)

Who taught her to depreciate thirteen dollars over 8 years, and who, anywhere in this country does this? Why did not Mr. I. M. Crackpot comment on some of these things? How could he bring himself not to find any error on her part? What does it mean that a cow barn is not a cow barn?

How is it that I had to suggest to her that the sale of long-term held timber is a capital sale? Why did she not find this herself, that is the error of my accountant treating it as ordinary income? Why did she not point out to me that my accountant had not taken a legitimate deduction for medical insurance? Why did she not find this herself rather than through me?

"$7.14" for a rented post hole digger for horses! I went to the rental agency myself to pick up this tool since the two workers had my sympathy digging through roots in the forest for the wintering area. "The expenses for the cattle were allowed in toto!" The post hole digger was itemized by her directly to horses but the wire on the inserted posts was ultimately assigned by some formula in part to cattle. That is a real novel accounting method! Shall I ask a question at this point or shall I substitute a word for an exclamation mark?

When my physician associate was shown the auditor's handling of telephone expenses under "horses or personal," he asked if we had talking horses on the farm. Enough is enough. There are too many to discuss.

It has been a little difficult to correspond with Mr. New C. Ants about tax matters since his letterheads have not borne an address until now, when he advises me not to send letters to him and Crackpot but to you. Since the post office is in such a mess and since he does not want me to write him anymore, perhaps you can advise his secretary to use the same rubber address stamp on the face of his franked envelopes in case they become lost.

My conviction grows strong that because others have compromised in regard to their farms, it was thought that myself would, and therefore this excuse for an audit was devised.

It is not my intent to seek general compromise. It is my intent to pay any just indebtedness as stated in February, 1969, 14 months ago. It is my intent to recover any just overpayment of taxes, two mentioned. There are others. I continue to predict as I also did in February, 1969, that the government will have wasted money again as it did for the audit of 1963, and the audit of 1964–1965, the latter of which you have previously seen.

District Director
A City, USA
Spring, 1965

KIND OF TAX: Income
TAXABLE YEAR: 1963

Dr. Roger Whitely and
   Mrs. Sarah Whitely
5000 15th Street
Pomona, Midamerica

Dear Dr. and Mrs. Whitely:

Our recent examination of your tax liability for the year indicated above discloses that no change is necessary to the tax reported. Accordingly the return will be accepted as filed.

Very truly yours,
Signature
District Director.

Sir, let us start fresh and realize that there may be three contestable points. These are:

  I. Is the farm horse truly a farm horse?

 II. How much of the cost of the farm improvements should be:

    (1) to pleasure horses?

    (2) to cattle?

III. After an acknowledgement by all of the actual cost of bedding and feeding a pleasure horse when labor is supplied free, then:

    (1) What is the excess amount of money, *if any,* taxpayers placed in their tax-deductible accounts inadvertently for

      (a) 1 pleasure horse in 1966 (child's pet)

      (b) 1 1/4 pleasure horses in 1967 (child's pet plus 1/4 horse)

      (c) 1 1/2 pleasure horses in 1968 (child's pet plus 1/2 horse)

How does the IRS treat a child's pleasure horse on thousands of other farms in this revenue district? Will the resulting treatment be equal for us and all others as equality is identified in our Constitution?

And it is known to me that I will swear that not one person who knows me whom I have asked to prepare a letter with affidavit or signature under a penalty of perjury, whether they work for the federal government or not, refused my request for assistance; but that there are only two groups from whom I have been unable to get testimony: (a) those who are employed in the Internal Revenue Service and (b) the fearless Fosdick I hired and to whom I had sent a retainer, when he changed his mind because of fear that the wrath of the IRS would fall next on him. In describing this episode to my first patient the following morning, she declared "That is frightening."

It should occur to both of us reasonable people that the first group is fearless and both second groups are fearful, one of truth and the other of potential punishment. Finally, perhaps at this conference we can together place prior court case decisions, which are enclosed, in their proper places in this argument.

Sir, I will contribute the best to my country that has contributed so much to me. But not one cent for tribute.

Chapter V

EPILOGUE

And now I tire and lay me down to sleep
For we fought the IRS whose hill was steep.
I wonder if then my slumbering soul they search
While I do nestle in warmth of perch?
For such six weeks I've never had
But when I awaken I'll be glad
To retaste the victory so very fine
No cancer left and all benign.
Will I dream of a directorship down the drain
Or cattle bellowing of branding pain?
Or of patients and people taking second seat
While I, gladiator, try for justice mete;
Or will it be of manure to move,
While quarantining vets so me behoove?
But where the workmen when I have need?
I beseech them all but none do heed.
Or will it be of new corporate enterprise?
Our family stockholders should not surmise
I think not of them at all.
Still, when I rise to her due call
I will all drop and court my spouse
Who must be thinking I'm a louse
For all this month I've said to her
What the deuce is omolene fer?

REFERENCES

Chapter I

1. Herman Melville, *Moby Dick* (1851), p. 39.
2. Samuel Johnson, *Boswell's Life of Johnson.*
3. Lord Hailsham, The *New York Times,* Oct. 16, 1960.
4. Rom. 7.7.
5. Eccl. 4.6.
6. Job 7.20.
7. Benjamin Franklin, "The Way to Wealth" (July 7, 1757), 1.
8. William Hazlitt, "On Pleasure of Painting," *Table Talk* (1821–22).
9. Horace, *Satires* (35–30 B.C.), 2.3.
10. Dwight D. Eisenhower, address to Republican National Committee, Jan. 31, 1958.
11. Baltasar Gracián, *The Art of Worldly Wisdom* (1647), p. 172, tr. Joseph Jacobs.
12. Emerson, "Compensation," *Essays: First Series* (1841).
13. Shakespeare, *Much Ado About Nothing* (1598-99), 3.-5.38.
14. Ps. 90.10.
15. *The Official Irish Joke Book* by Harry Wilde, Pinnacle Books, N.Y.C. pp. 102–3.
16. Maxim Gorky, *Enemies* (1906) p. 2.
17. Shakespeare, *Othello.*
18. Lord Kilmuir, *Political Adventure.*
19. Will Rogers, *The Autobiography of Will Rogers* (1949), p. 19.

20. Mark Twain, "Pudd'nhead Wilson's New Calendar," *Following the Equator* (1897), 8.
21. Mary McCarthy, "America the Beautiful: The Humanist in the Bathtub," *On the Contrary* (1961).
22. Ps. 55.21.
23. Matt. 9.11–12.
24. Mahatma Gandhi.
25. Shakespeare, *The Merchant of Venice*.
26. A. J. Ayer, *Essay on Humanism*.
27. Blaise Pascal, *Pensées*.
28. Benjamin Franklin, *Poor Richard's Almanack* (1732–57).
29. *The Official Jewish Joke Book* by Larry Wilde, p. 21, Pinnacle Books, N.Y.C.
30. Ibid., p. 36.
31. Arabic Proverb.
32. Martin Luther King.
33. Eccl. 4.23.
34. Molière, Preface to *Tartuffe* (1664), tr. John Wood.
35. W. R. Inge, *Personal Religion and the Life of Devotion*.
36. St. Thomas Aquinas.
37. André Malraux, *L'Espoir* (1937), 22.12.
38. Isa. 52.7.
39. *The Polish Joke Book,* p. 12. Edited by Mike Kowalski, Belmont Tower Books, N.Y.C.

Chapter II

1. Nicholas Murray Butler.
2. *The Polish Joke Book,* p. 32. Edited by Mike Kowalski, Belmont Tower Books, N.Y.C.
3. Wis. 17.12.
4. Isa. 59.14.

Chapter III

1. Rom. 1.22.
2. Prov. 12.23.

3. Matt. 15.14.

4. *The Polish Joke Book.* p. 80. Edited by Mike Kowalski, Belmont Tower Books, N.Y.C.

5. Law of John Peckham.

6. Aristotle, *Nicomachean Ethics* (4th C. B.C.), 2.9, tr. J. A. K. Thomson.

7. Pietro Aretino, letter to Girolamo Quirini, Nov. 21, 1953, tr. Samuel Putnam.

8. Henry Ward Beecher, *Proverbs from Plymouth Pulpit* (1887).

9. Finley Peter Dunne, "On Golf," *Mr. Dooley on Making a Will* (1919).

10. Mark Twain, "Pudd'nhead Wilson's Calendar," *Pudd'nhead Wilson* (1894), p. 10.

11. *The Official Irish Joke Book*, p. 37, by Larry Wilde, Pinnacle Books, N.Y.C.

12. 2 Tim. 42.

13. Richard Whately, *Apophthegms.*

Chapter IV

1. Williams Collins, *Persian Eclogues* (1742), 2.

2. Epictetus, *Discourses* (2nd c.), 1.2, tr. Thomas W. Higginson.

3. Thomas Fuller, M.D., *Gnomologia* (1732) 5088.

4. Philip Rieff, preface to *Freud: The Mind of the Moralist* (1959).

5. Eccl. 3.13.

6. Ovid, *Love's Cure* (c. A.D. 8), tr. J. Lewis May.

7. Publilius Syrus, *Moral Sayings* (1st c. B.C.), 201, tr. Darius Lyman.

8. *The Official Jewish Joke Book*, p. 89. Larry Wilde, Pinnacle Books, N.Y.C.

9. Maxim Gorky, *The Lower Depths* (1903), p. 4, tr. Alexander Bakshy.

10. *The Official Irish Joke Book*, p. 20. Larry Wilde, Pinnacle Books, N.Y.C.

11. John Dryden, *The Hind and the Panther* (1687), 11.239.
12. Hindustani Proverb, Quoted in Sir Winston Churchill's *While England Slept,* 1936.
13. James Madison, speech, Virginia Convention, June 16, 1788.
14. Napoleon I, *Maxims* (1804–15).
15. James T. Rapier, *Congressional Globe,* 1873.
16. Samuel Johnson, quoted in Boswell's *Life of Samuel Johnson,* April 6, 1775.
17. Omar Khayyam: *Rubaiyat.*
18. Joseph Kraft, Editorial writer, Publishers-Hall Syndicate, Mar. 23, 1970.
19. Matt. 6.28–29.
20. *Webster's New American Dictionary,* 1966, Books, Inc., Publishers.
21. Editorial. April 1, 1970.
22. Jas. 4.7.
23. Ronald Knox, *Let Dons Delight.*
24. Prov. 26.20.
25. Captain Eddie Rickenbacker, Conference of the Texas Medical Association, Jan. 20, 1962.